P9-CJL-420

THE BIOGRAPHY OF

Ancient Israel

Contraversions

Critical Studies in Jewish Literature, Culture, and Society

Daniel Boyarin and Chana Kronfeld, General Editors

1. *A Radical Jew: Paul and the Politics of Identity*, by Daniel Boyarin
2. *On the Margins of Modernism: Decentering Literary Dynamics*, by Chana Kronfeld
3. *Crossing the Jabbok: Illness and Death in Ashkenazi Judaism in Sixteenth- through Nineteenth-Century Prague*, by Sylvie-Anne Goldberg, translated by Carol Cosman
4. *Foregone Conclusions: Against Apocalyptic History*, by Michael André Bernstein
5. *Founder of Hasidism: A Quest for the Historical Ba'al Shem Tov*, by Moshe Rosman
6. *Conversations with Dvora: An Experimental Biography of the First Modern Hebrew Woman Writer*, by Amia Lieblich, translated by Naomi Seidman
7. *A Marriage Made in Heaven: The Sexual Politics of Hebrew and Yiddish*, by Naomi Seidman
8. *Unheroic Conduct: The Rise of Heterosexuality and the Invention of the Jewish Man*, by Daniel Boyarin
9. *Spinning Fantasies: Rabbis, Gender, and History*, by Miriam Peskowitz
10. *Black Fire on White Fire: An Essay on Jewish Hermeneutics, from Midrash to Kabbalah*, by Betty Rojtman, translated by Steven Rendall
11. *The Dispersion of Egyptian Jewry: Culture, Politics, and the Formation of a Modern Diaspora*, by Joel Beinin
12. *Booking Passage: Exile and Homecoming in the Modern Jewish Imagination*, by Sidra Dekoven Ezrahi
13. *The Hyena People: Ethiopian Jews in Christian Ethiopia*, by Hagar Salamon
14. *The Biography of Ancient Israel: National Narratives in the Bible*, by Ilana Pardes

For Steve
with esteem

THE BIOGRAPHY OF

Ancient Israel

NATIONAL NARRATIVES IN THE BIBLE

Ilana Pardes

UNIVERSITY OF CALIFORNIA PRESS

Berkeley   Los Angeles   London

The publisher gratefully acknowledges the generous contributions to this book from the David B. Gold Foundation, the Lucius N. Littauer Foundation, and the Skirball Foundation.

University of California Press
Berkeley and Los Angeles, California

University of California Press, Ltd.
London, England

Library of Congress Cataloging-in-Publication Data

Pardes, Ilana.
The biography of ancient Israel: national narratives in the Bible / Ilana Pardes.
p. cm. — (Contraversions ; 14)
Includes bibliographical references and index.
ISBN 0-520-21110-3 (alk. paper)
1. Bible. O.T. Pentateuch—Historiography. 2. Bible as literature. 3. Bible. O.T. Pentateuch—History of Biblical events. 4. Jewish nationalism. I. Title. II. Series.
BS1225.5.P37 2000
296.3'1172—dc21 99-27865
CIP

Manufactured in the United States of America

08 07 06 05 04 03 02 01 00
10 9 8 7 6 5 4 3 2 1

The paper used in this publication meets the minimum requirements of ANSI/NISO Z39.48-1992 (R 1997) (*Permanence of Paper*). ♾

In memory of my father, Don Patinkin,
and for my son, Eyal

CONTENTS

ACKNOWLEDGMENTS

This book wandered from station to station with the help of so many. I have benefited immeasurably from the inspiring suggestions and radiant thought of Ruth Nevo. I cannot imagine what this national biography would have looked like without her ongoing enthusiasm and encouragement. I am very grateful to Moshe Halbertal and Zali Gurevich, who gave so generously of their time from the moment of departure on, reading one chapter after another, enriching the voyage with their superb insights and criticism. I have been fortunate to have had many other readers at different junctures: Elizabeth Abel, Robert Alter, Jessica Bonn, Michal Ben-Naphtali, Alon Confino, Ruth Ginsburg, Miki Gluzman, Erich Gruen, Galit Hasan-Rokem, Moshe Greenberg, Melila Helner-Eshed, Francis Landy, Menahem Lurberboim, Adi Ophir, Michele Rosenthal, Naomi Seidman, Michael Walzer, and Shira Wolosky.

I wish to thank my friends and colleagues in the Department of Comparative Literature at the Hebrew University of Jerusalem for providing me with such a supportive intellectual home. I am also indebted to my astute students at Jerusalem and at the University of California, Berkeley (where I spent a sabbatical in fall 1996), who contributed to my understanding of national imagination in the Bible through their comments and critiques.

I owe much to the editors of this series, Chana Kronfeld and Daniel Boyarin, for their fruitful suggestions and unstinting belief in the project. My thanks to Doug Abrams Arava and to Reed Malcolm at the University of California Press for their expert guidance and devotion. Earlier versions of two chapters in this book have been published previously: chapter 2 in *Comparative Literature* 49, no. 1 (Winter 1997); chapter 5 in *History and Memory* 6, no. 2 (Fall–Winter 1994).

The Federman Grant of the Hebrew University provided funds to support my research. I have also had the privilege of being a fellow at the Shalom Hartman Institute for Advanced Studies in the past two years and am grateful for this stimulating context. Special thanks to Moshe Idel for his generosity and admirable interpretive openness.

My family has been an unending source of love and encouragement. I am indebted to my husband, Itamar Lurie, for his patience, abiding faith, and for long, illuminating conversations on psychoanalytic theory. I owe much to Keren, my daughter, for her remarkable exuberance and thoughtful questions. This book is dedicated to the memory of my father, Don Patinkin, who gave me the map of wanderings (reproduced on the jacket), long before I began to write on it; who taught me so much about thinking, reading, and writing, though our fields were so different. This book is also dedicated to Eyal, my son, who was born in the initial stages of writing and gave me invaluable power ever since.

CHAPTER ONE

Introduction

Split Conception

In a grand annunciation scene, hovering between dream and revelation, God leads Abraham outdoors and says, "Look now toward heaven, and tell the stars, if thou be able to number them. . . . So shall thy seed be" (Gen. 15:5).[1] To envision an abstract concept such as nation requires poetic power, a metaphoric leap that would make the transition from one to a multitude more tangible. Abraham, at this point in his life, finds it difficult to imagine even the birth of a single heir (old and childless as he is), but God demands that he step out of the tent into the night and envision the coming birth of an entire nation. The sight of stars sown in the vast expanses of the sky is construed as a key to understanding the future image of Abraham's seed. But much remains unknown. The metaphor does not solve the riddle of the nation to be but rather opens it through a broadening of horizons.[2] God challenges Abraham to count the stars only to prove that it is an impossible task, for the stars reveal themselves as unfathomable, infinite. The stars, however, are but a preliminary guiding metaphor.

The central metaphor for the nation in the Bible turns out to be less glittering and more complicated: the nation is predominantly imagined as a person.

The history of the children of Israel, I propose, is shaped as a biography. The nation—especially in Exodus and Numbers where the primary questions about the origin and singularity of the nation are raised—is personified; it is a character with a distinct voice (represented at times in a singular mode); it moans and groans, is euphoric at times, complains frequently, and rebels against Moses and God time and again. It has a collective body—a heart that needs to be circumcised (Deut. 30:6) and, above all, a stiff, unyielding neck (Exod. 32). Israel has a life story: it was conceived in the days of Abraham; its miraculous birth took place with the Exodus, the parting of the Red Sea; then came a long period of childhood and restless adolescence in the wilderness; and finally adulthood was approached with the conquest of Canaan.

The relevance of metaphor to the construction of nations has been raised in the groundbreaking work of Benedict Anderson. A nation is necessarily imagined, he claims, because it consists of numerous members who do not know each other yet share "the image of their communion."[3] Anderson is particularly intrigued by the capacity of national imaginings to create a sense of unity and continuity at points of clear disjunction. One of his examples—which is most relevant to my own project—is the question of national biographies. In the rich, though brief, concluding section of *Imagined Communities,* Anderson argues that nations, much like individuals, generate biographies.[4] Births of nations are not as easily identifiable, not to mention their deaths, but the two modes of biographical narratives share much in common. Above all, they both attempt to smooth out the fragmentary and slippery qualities of memory as they fashion a conception of identity.

I take the concept of "national biography" from the margins of Anderson's work and place it at the center of attention, opening it up to further reflection. I do so while introducing this concept into new realms. First, my study moves beyond the framework of political thought (Anderson's main concern is the origin and spread of nationalism) into the field of literary studies. I focus on the *textual* manifestations of the metaphor, the network of anthropomorphisms by which a collective character named "Israel" springs to life. I explore the representation of communal motives, hidden desires, collective anxieties, the drama and suspense embedded in each phase of the nation's life: from birth in exile through suckling in the wilderness to a long process of maturation that has no definite end. Second, I shift the discussion on the fashioning of individual and collective identities from modern times to the ancient world.

Like most recent scholars of nationhood, Anderson regards the nation as a modern phenomenon, dating back to the Enlightenment. He rightly insists on the historicity of the nation in his critique of previous perceptions of national identity as natural and universal. Yet by limiting the scope of the much-needed historical examination of the phenomenon, he overlooks the fascinating manifestations of the shaping of national identities in earlier periods.[5] The "nation" (far more than the "city" or "clan") is the primary category for mapping the world in the Bible. The Bible's perception in this respect, as Jacob Licht suggests, is closer to nineteenth-century Europe than to feudal Europe in the Middle Ages. The Table of Nations in Genesis 10 offers a genealogy of seventy different peoples—from Greece and Crete through Cush and Egypt to Canaan, Babylon, and Ashur—who "branched out" on the earth after the Flood. The following episode—the story of the Tower of Babel—provides an etiological tale regarding the origin of national diversity. Humankind was once one, we are told, "and the whole earth was of one language, and of one speech" (Gen. 11:1). But the people set out to build a tower "whose top may reach into heaven," challenging the demarcation between the human and the divine realms. God's response was to confound their language and to scatter them upon the face of the earth. Interestingly enough, the story of the Tower of Babel, where the formation of nations is tied to linguistic splitting, calls to mind Anderson's suggestion that the rise of the nation in Europe was enhanced by the decline of Latin as the language of a "pan-European high intelligentsia" and the growing power of the vernacular languages.[6]

To be sure, ancient Israel is not a nation-state, nor can one speak of nationalism or sovereignty in this connection (though freedom is part and parcel of national awakening in the Bible). Israel is God's nation, and God has the right and power to destroy it and create another nation instead—in fact, He comes close to doing so at several points.[7] And yet the intriguing questions put forth by Anderson—How are nations imagined? What are the strategies by which national memory is constructed? How is a sense of national belonging created?—are most relevant to the shaping of the biography of ancient Israel.

I do not mean to suggest that national literatures were common in the ancient world. Israel's preoccupation with its reason for being is exceptional in the ancient Near East.[8] In Greece and particularly in Rome, however, narratives concerning national origins are equally important.[9] Erich Gruen provides an insightful analysis of the formation of Roman national identity against the background of Greek culture. Gruen examines such key cultural developments as the choice to adopt the legend of Troy as a legend of origin. "It enabled Rome to associate itself with the rich and complex fabric of Hellenic tradition. . . . But at the same time, it also announced Rome's distinctiveness from that world."[10] Israel's history bears resemblance to the Roman one. It too involves a divine Promise, individuation from a major civilization, a quest for lost roots, a long journey to what is construed as the land of the forefathers, and a gory conquest.[11]

What makes the Bible unique is the extent to which it relies on the personification and dramatization of the nation. In the *Aeneid*, by way of comparison, the plot revolves around Aeneas. The wanderings between Troy and the promised new land are primarily Aeneas's wanderings: the people remain a rather pale foil. They engage in no conflict—whether with Aeneas or with the gods—that would grant them access to the central stage. The biblical text is significantly different in its rendering of national drama. Israel is a protagonist whose moves and struggles determine the map—so much so that forty years of wanderings in the desert are added to the itinerary as a result of the people's preference of Egypt over Canaan.

The fashioning of Israel as a character is a forceful unifying strategy, but the metaphor does not yield a homogeneous account of national formation. The biblical text reveals points of tension between different traditions regarding the nation's history and character. Even the nation's sexual identity is not stable. While the Pentateuch shapes a male character, referring to the people as *'am* (singular masculine noun), the Prophets, more often than not, represent Israel as female, using "Jerusalem" or "Zion" (feminine nouns) as alternative national designations. Much like Virginia Woolf's reconstruction of English history in *Orlando*, biblical historiography relies on a complex gendered approach in its representation of the nation, allowing shifts between sexual roles as well as a more open and flexible definition of masculine and feminine identities.[12]

This book focuses on the intricacies of national imagination in the Pentateuch and as such deals with the construction of a male character who is marked as God's firstborn son.[13] Double personification is at stake—of God and the nation—creating a familial link between the two.[14] If Rome's sacred origin is assured through the divine blood of its founding fathers—Aeneas, as one recalls, is Venus's son, and Romulus and Remus are the offspring of Mars—in the case of Israel, the nation as a whole, metaphorically speaking, is God's son.[15] On sending Moses to Pharaoh to deliver the people, God proclaims: "Israel is my son, even my firstborn. And I say unto thee [Pharaoh], Let my son go" (Exod. 4:23). The priority given to Israel by the Father represents a translation into national terms of the reversal of the primogeniture law—a phenomenon so central in the lives of the patriarchs. The late-born nation that came "to the stage after all its neighbors had assumed their historical roles" is elevated by God to the position of the chosen firstborn.[16]

Israel is a chosen nation, God's nation, but the reason for its chosenness remains obscure. It does not succeed in following traditional norms of male heroism, nor does it become an exemplary nation with high moral and religious standards. The more mature Israel, in the plains of Moab, on the threshold of Canaan, is a far more established community than the nascent nation on the way out of Egypt, but this by no means suggests an advance in spirituality. Whereas in the initial stages of the journey the children of Israel worship the Golden Calf in a carnivalesque feast, at the last station, just before crossing the Jordan River, they "cling" to Baal Peor (under the influence of Moabite women), replacing Egyptian religious practices with Canaanite ones. The Song of Moses, with its synoptic presentation of Israel's history, regards the nation as an ungrateful son whose conduct fails to improve over time: "Do ye thus requite the Lord, O foolish people and unwise? Is not he thy father that hath . . . made thee, and established thee?" (Deut. 32:6). Instead of appreciating God's vigilance, Moses claims, once the nation grew and "waxed fat" it did not hesitate to "kick" (Deut. 32:15).

What fascinates me most in the primary biography of ancient Israel is the ambivalence that lies at its very base, an ambivalence that is expressed so poignantly through the intense struggles between the Father (or Moses) and His people. The nation is both the chosen son and the rebel son, and accordingly its relationship with the Father is at once intimate and strained. While the biblical text presents this ambivalence primarily from the divine parental perspective, I will devote no less attention to the fragmentary and somewhat cryptic vox populi. I read the "stiff neck" of the "son" against the grain, probing the murmurings of the people, fleshing out their critique of the official parental line. I regard the people's insistence on remembering Egypt as a land of pleasures, their questioning of the official perception of Canaan as homeland, and their desire for syncretic modes of religious practice as vital countertrends in the nation's biography.

Let me emphasize that the fictional quality of the struggle between God and the nation does not preclude the historicity of the text. Israel's beginning, as Amos Funkenstein observes, is situated in "historical times"—in the days of the Exodus—rather than in a mythical "in illo tempore."[17] Similarly, God defines Himself, at Sinai and elsewhere, as the one who brought Israel out of Egypt—not as the Creator of primeval times. Even at moments when the biography of ancient Israel relies on mythical materials—primarily, on the myth of the birth of the hero and the myth of the hero's return—these are inextricably connected with a historiographical drive to record memorable past events and question their meaning. In the Bible, history and literature go hand in hand, more explicitly than in modern historiography, which is why it serves as a paradigmatic case for the examination of the narrative base of national constructions.[18]

Coming from literature, however, I am primarily concerned with the textuality of history rather than with speculations about the historical contexts against which these biblical events took place. The New Historicism has taught us the value of foregrounding the representational practices of historical documents. Stephen Greenblatt's *Marvelous Possessions*—with its exploration of the literary aspects of the European reports on the New World—is exemplary in this respect. The different biblical accounts of the nation's past require similar consideration.

Literary critics of the Bible have tended to avoid Exodus and Numbers, not to mention Deuteronomy. They marveled at the complex rendering of individual characters and left the nation to the historians.[19] "How fraught with background . . . are characters like Saul and David! How entangled and stratified are such human relations as those between David and Absalom, between David and Joab!" exclaims Erich Auerbach, passionately, in his wonderful essay on biblical style.[20] The psychological depth—

"the simultaneous existence of various layers of consciousness"—that Auerbach attributes to individual figures is no less intriguing in the case of the nation.[21] The silences underlying the "background" of Israel's representation, the suggestive influence of the unexpressed, the intensity of immeasurable despair and joy, the entangled relations between the nation and God, between Israel and other nations—all "demand interpretation."[22]

My analysis of the psychological dimension of Israel's character is indebted to Freud's *Moses and Monotheism.* In this work, Freud offers a fascinating account of Israel's origins that entails an application of his observations regarding the individual to what he calls "mass psychology." Designating Moses as the founding father of the nation, he uncovers a collective Oedipal drama in the biblical text. Moses, he conjectures, was not a Hebrew but an Egyptian. More specifically, he was an Egyptian noble who believed in the monotheism established by Ikhnaton. In an attempt to save the Aton religion (with its exclusive worship of the sun-power) from extinction, Moses sought to pass on its principles to the oppressed Hebrews. But the mass of liberated slaves did not accept the rigid exigencies of the Mosaic faith and killed the national father in an unrecorded revolt. The traces of this traumatic murder, however, did not disappear, nor was the memory of Moses wholly forgotten. Over a period of centuries, the "memory traces" of the Mosaic tradition took part in "the formation of a national character" and eventually acquired enough force among the Hebrews to "return" as the exclusive religion of biblical Israel.[23]

Freud's *Moses and Monotheism* is surely a wild and speculative rendition of Israelite history, for which he was criticized from the moment of publication.[24] And yet it provides important insights with respect to biblical historiography and national formation. It provides, as Yosef Hayim Yerushalmi argues, "a singular vision of history as essentially a story of remembering and forgetting." What has been overlooked, Yerushalmi goes on to claim, "is how strangely analogous it is . . . to the biblical conception of history, where the continual oscillation of memory and forgetting is a major theme through all the narratives of historical events."[25] I would add that what has also been overlooked is the extent to which Freud here is attentive to the Bible's *own* preoccupation with the interrelation between individual and collective histories, between individual and collective fantasies and traumas.

Freud sheds much light on the ambivalence and violence that characterize the father-son relationship in the Pentateuch, though he never engages in a textual analysis of the metaphors at stake. What his work, however, neglects to consider is the impact of the repression and loss of the heavenly Mother on the shaping of Israel's history. To be sure, the nation's Mother does not appear explicitly in the biography of ancient Israel—this is precisely one of the peculiar features of this biography—but the traces of her milk, I believe, may be found in the wilderness. Relying on the insightful work of Melanie Klein, I follow these traces and reflect on the different aspects of a more primary collective drama—that of suckling and weaning. National ambivalence is not only directed vis-à-vis the Father but also in relation to an absent Mother whose vigilance is desperately sought.

The limits of the metaphor should be noted. I do not postulate identity between the individual psyche and the nation's "psyche" (as Freud does). A collective character is necessarily more heterogeneous and less predictable. The Pentateuch's story of national development resists clear-cut boundaries between different phases in the nation's life history. Roughly speaking, chronology is maintained, and yet images of national birth, youth, initiation, and suckling intermingle throughout. Thus the distinct manifestation of national suckling appears only in Numbers 11, where Moses likens the people to a suckling infant in the wilderness, long after the grand-scale initiation at Sinai. But, after all, such boundaries are never that clear in individual biographies either. Infantile dreams may linger on and initiation is rarely exhausted in one rite. A youth is also something of a child, or an infant being weaned, or even an infant just born—all the more so in the biblical context where the word *na'ar* may mean "youth," "child," and occasionally "infant."[26]

My work, then, is more archaeological than it may seem at first. I reconstruct a linear story out of scattered metaphors and intermingled images. At times, I go so far as to uncover the figurative base of episodes that do not rely explicitly on metaphors; that is, I juxtapose explicit anthropomorphisms with implicit ones. In other instances, my reconstruction of a given phase in Israel's life is sharpened via a comparison with analogous moments in the lives of paradigmatic individual characters—primarily Moses and Jacob—whose histories shed light on the nation's route.

Between the Parts

I would like to return, by way of conclusion, to my point of departure: the initial imaginings of Israel in Genesis. Israel is not yet a character in Genesis, but this book serves as an essential introduction to the nation's biography. It is here that the primary features of the nation are first conceived. Central concepts such as chosenness and covenant are set forth as the borders of the Promised Land are outlined. But Genesis, interestingly enough, not only fashions national constructs: it also considers their instability, the extent to which communities may be fractured and displaced.[27] The shadow of exile falls upon Israel's history from the moment of conception. Even before Abraham's seed actually appears on the horizon it is destined to be scattered elsewhere. Dreams of national grandeur blend with nightmares of dispersion. Right after the ceremonial annunciation of the nation's birth through the promising sight of the stars in the sky, God addresses Abraham once again in the memorable episode of the covenant of the parts:

> And he said unto him, I am the Lord that brought thee out of Ur of the Chaldees, to give thee this land to inherit it. And he said, Lord God, whereby shall I know that I shall inherit it? And he said unto him, Take me an heifer of three years old, and a she goat of three years old, and a ram of three years old, and a turtledove, and a young pigeon. And he took unto him all these, and divided them in the midst, and laid each piece one against another: but the birds divided he not. And when the fowls came down upon the carcases, Abram drove them away. And when the sun was going down, a deep sleep fell upon Abram; and, lo, an horror of great darkness fell upon him. And he said unto Abram, Know of a surety that thy seed shall be a stranger in a land that is not theirs, and shall serve them; and they shall afflict them four hundred years; And also that nation, whom they shall serve, will I judge: and afterward shall they come out with great sub-

> stance. . . . But in the fourth generation they shall come hither again: for the iniquity of the Amorites is not yet full. And it came to pass, that, when the sun went down, and it was dark, behold a smoking furnace, and a burning lamp [torch] that passed between those pieces. (Gen. 15:7–17)

The scene between the severed animal parts is a perplexing mystery that calls for symbolic readings. Relying on covenantal documents in the ancient Near East and in Greece, biblical scholars have suggested that such rituals are meant to prevent transgressions, the underlying idea being that the fate of the party who ventures to violate the covenant will be like that of the severed animals.[28] The Hebrew expression *karat berit*, literally, to "cut a covenant" (see Gen. 15:18), may reinforce this notion. Such legal background accentuates the total commitment demanded by God from the chosen ones—first from Abraham and later from his descendants—but it does not take into consideration the interrelations between the different elements of the scene.

The image of the cut carcasses attacked by carrion birds seems to serve as a visual prefiguration to the troubling future God discloses on this occasion.[29] Abraham, as it were, envisions the fractures and affliction that await his offspring an instant before a "deep sleep" falls upon him, an instant before God foretells the nation's future exile to him explicitly in a troubling dream. He senses the "horror of great darkness" (*'eiyma chashekha gedola*), of four hundred years of servitude in a "strange land," through his struggle to drive off the ominous carrion birds. "Carcasses," *pegarim*, is a term that is primarily used to depict human bodies. Is its appearance here an indication that human lives are at stake?

The first patriarch falls asleep only to discover that the boundaries between dream and reality are blurred, for the dream is as nightmarish, at first, as the sight that precedes it.

God's oneiric prophecy reveals an unsettling overlap between the chosen and the nonchosen. The fate of the Israelites is not radically different from that of other communities. Their chosenness does not exempt them from spending many years in the lowly position of oppressed exiles, nor does it assure their unconditional possession of the Promised Land. Israel, apparently, is not the only nation on God's mind. The divine plan takes into consideration other peoples as well, which is why the return of Israel to its land will depend, among other things, on the moral conduct of the Amorites. The Amorites have the right to reside in Canaan until their "iniquity" is "full."[30] Only then will God deliver Abraham's descendants out of bondage and lead them back to Canaan. Here, as elsewhere in Genesis, divine promises turn out to be rather fragile: their fulfillment is continually deferred as their significance becomes more baffling.

But then a smoking brazier appears suddenly with a wondrous flaming torch that passes between the pieces—a precursor to the pillar of fire? A "forelighting" of the nation's passage between parted waters in the Red Sea?[31] The redemptive firelight that flashes up in the after-sunset darkness endows the evasive oracular promises of the dream with strange force. There is a sign of life among the parts after all. Exile, it seems, is not the end of the story but rather a point of departure.[32] Much as Abraham's story begins with a dramatic departure (from Ur)—as God reminds him in the initial exchange (15:7)—so the nation's story begins with exile and a spectacular exodus (the same verb "to bring out," *lehotsi*, is used in both contexts). If other nations rely on autochthonous myths, the Bible insists on Israel's position as outsider in relation to its land.[33] Ancient Israel was born in exile, way down in Egypt, far from the site of conception, far away from its destined homeland. Such displacement, however, is construed as an essential rift in the nation's biography, as if the journey through the land of the other were indispensable to the emergence of Israel as character.[34]

CHAPTER TWO

Imagining the Birth of a Nation

The metaphor of national birth is probably the most resonant anthropomorphic image in national biographies from antiquity to modern times. In fact, it is so resonant one tends to forget that nations are not born literally but rather are imagined in these terms. Every nation, however, has its own birth story, or birth stories. The Book of Exodus provides an intriguingly complex representation of Israel's birth in keeping with the preliminary imaginings of the nation in Genesis. The opening verses of Exodus 1 make clear that God's reiterated promises to Abraham, Isaac, and Jacob—the grand national annunciation scenes of Genesis—are finally realized. The descendants of Jacob, whose names are listed solemnly, multiply at an uncanny pace and turn into a "mighty" nation: the nation of the "children of Israel."[1] "Israel" for the first time is not merely Jacob's second, elevated, name but rather a collective designation of a burgeoning community that "fills" the land. But then we discover that God's darker prophecy, in the covenant of the parts, is equally fulfilled: Israel is born in a prolonged exile against Pharaonic bondage.

Representing the birth of a nation is not a simple task. Let me suggest that the imagining of this dramatic event in Exodus is facilitated by the interweaving of two biographies: the story of the birth of Moses and that of the nation.[2] The fashioning of Israel as character, here as elsewhere, is inseparable from a complementary narrative strategy: the marking of individuals whose histories are paradigmatic. The nation's life story, in other words, is modeled in relation to the biographies of select characters.[3] We have already noticed the national dimension inscribed in Abraham's story: the fashioning of his departure from Ur as prefiguration of the nation's exodus. Abraham, however, is only the first exemplary figure.[4] The heterogeneity of national imagination in the Bible depends on a variety of representatives. Fragments of the biographies of Isaac, of Jacob, the eponymous father, and even of Hagar, the Egyptian handmaid, whose affliction foreshadows the nation's enslavement in Egypt, are also linked in different ways to the nation's biography and take part in its construction.[5]

On the question of birth, Moses' biography is of special importance. The analogy between the one and the multitude in this case is more immediate. Unlike the patriarchal biographies that pertain to a distant past and flicker over the chasm of time, Moses' story is fashioned within the same historical setting. Moses is a national leader whose history blends with the history of the nation. He is one of many Hebrew babies persecuted by Pharaoh. His story, however, is marked as the exemplary account that sheds light on the collective birth story as it prefigures the deliverance of the nation as a whole from bondage.

Moses' birth story, as Otto Rank aptly suggests in *The Myth of the Birth of the Hero*, shares much in common with mythical birth stories. What characterizes the birth of a hero? Rank offers a list of recurrent motifs, relying on a variety of myths—from the birth legend of Saragon, the third-millennium B.C.E. king of Akkad, to the renowned story of Oedipus's exposure and the tale of Remus and Romulus, the legendary founders of Rome.[6] The conception of the hero, he claims, is usually impeded by difficulties such as abstinence or prolonged barrenness. During or before pregnancy there is a prophecy, or an oracle cautioning the father against the hero's birth; the father tries to shape a different future and gives orders to kill his newborn son; the babe is then placed in a basket or a box and delivered to the waves. Against all odds, however, the hero is saved by animals or by lowly people and is suckled by a female animal or by a humble woman. When full-grown, he discovers his royal parents, takes revenge on his father, and, recognized by his people, finally achieves rank and honors.[7]

Following Freud, Rank reads the myth as an expression of Oedipal struggles between fathers and sons. The hero is he who is capable of standing against his father and overcoming him. The myth traces this struggle "back to the very dawn of the hero's life, by having him born against his father's will and saved in spite of his father's evil intentions."[8] What we have here in Freudian terms is a "family romance," the kind of story a child fabricates when feeling deserted. Resentful of his parents' neglect (opportunities arise only too often), the child thinks of himself as a foundling, an adopted child, whose true parents—royal, needless to say—will eventually be revealed.[9]

Moses' story is indeed compatible in many ways with Rank's model: a threatened child, the exposure in the basket, the miraculous deliverance of the foundling, the two sets of parents, and the final acknowledgment of the hero's power. But then there is a significant difference that Rank smooths over by claiming that the original story had been distorted by the biblical scribes: Moses' true parents are not the royal ones but rather the poor Hebrew slaves.

What Rank overlooks—as does Freud in the opening section of *Moses and Monotheism*—is that at a moment of national birth the inversion of the two sets of parents is purposeful. Moses' "true" parents are higher in rank despite their lowly position precisely because they are members of the chosen nation to be. This lapse in their readings of Moses' story derives in part from their failure to see the relevance of the myth to the representation of the nation as a whole.

The juxtaposition of Moses' story and that of the nation entails an adaptation of the myth of the birth of the hero on a national plane. Put differently, it enables the construction of a myth of the birth of the nation. Israel's birth, much like that of Moses, takes place against Pharaoh's will.

> And the children of Israel were fruitful, and increased abundantly, and multiplied, and waxed exceeding mighty; and the land was filled with them. Now there arose up a new king over Egypt, which knew not Joseph. And he said unto his people, Behold, the people of the children of Israel are more and mightier than we. (Exod. 1:8–9)

Interestingly, the expression *'am beney yisrael*, "the nation of the children of Israel," is first used by none other than Pharaoh. Pharaoh's anxieties over the safety of his rule enable him to perceive the rise of Israel long before the Hebrews themselves can. Intimidated by the uncanny growth of the Hebrews, Pharaoh orders that every son who is born shall be cast into the Nile "and every daughter ye shall save alive" (Exod. 1:22). Much has been written about his curious choice to get rid of the male babies alone but with no consideration of the mythical background.[10] What is at stake here is an application of the exposure motif (a male motif to begin with) to a community of sons. Pharaoh, the ruler of the parent-nation, fears the power of a budding nation of rivals growing within Egypt. Parental anxieties—what will emerge from the teeming womb?—thus conflate with racist anxieties—will the others overbear?

Shiphrah and Puah, the two midwives whose names are associated with "beauty" (the former) and "birth sighs" (the latter), are the national correlate of Moses' female deliverers in Exodus 2.[11] Here too a curious detail in the text—the fact that two midwives are considered sufficient for a national massacre—can be explained in terms of the mythical context and the interrelations of the two biographies. The midwives, much like humble rescuers of heroes, choose to violate the king's decree and save the threatened newborns. They trick Pharaoh by telling him midwives' tales: "And the king of Egypt called for the midwives, and said unto them, Why have ye done this thing, and have saved the men children alive? And the midwives said unto Pharaoh, Because the Hebrew women are not as the Egyptian women; for they are lively, and are delivered ere the midwives come in unto them" (1:18–19). Shiphrah and Puah outwit Pharaoh by confirming his racist anxieties concerning the proliferation of the Hebrew slaves. Relying on a common racist notion, according to which the other is closer to Nature, they claim that the Hebrew women need no midwives, for unlike Egyptian women, they are animal-like (*ki chayot hena*) and can give birth without professional help. There is an outburst of vitality out there, they seem to suggest, that cannot be yoked to the legal apparatus of the Pharaonic court. The recurrence of the term "midwife" in this brief episode—it appears seven times—highlights the admirable power and courage of the two women.

The Politics of Birth

So far I have underlined the mythical qualities of the representation of the nation's birth, but one needs to bear in mind the ways in which myth here is set against the historical setting of slavery, or rather against slave narratives whose purpose is to document the concrete horrors of bondage and commemorate modes of resistance. Michael Walzer offers a cogent reading of the Egyptian oppression in his meditation on the political meanings of the Exodus. He defines the enslavement in Egypt as a form of cruel tyranny, exercised from the seat of political power, that insisted not only on making a profit through forced labor but also on crushing the slaves' spirits, on embittering their lives with humiliating work.[12] Indeed, the Hebrews could not at first listen to Moses' revolutionary ideas "for anguish of spirit, and for cruel bondage" (Exod. 6:9). The Hebrew is *kotser ruach*, literally, "shortness of spirit," an idiom for impatience, but in this context it acquires, Walzer claims, the additional meaning of "dispiritedness."[13]

What needs to be added to Walzer's analysis is a consideration of the ways in which bondage distorts and undermines the process of reproduction. The phenomenon is all too well known from testimonies regarding other instances of slavery. Bartolomé de Las Casas's depiction of New World slavery is relevant in this connection:

> Thus husbands and wives were together once every eight or ten months, and when they met they were so exhausted and depressed on both sides that they had no mind for marital intercourse, and in this way they ceased to procreate. As for the newly born, they died early because their mothers overworked and famished, had no milk to nurse them with, and for this reason, while I was in Cuba, 7000 children died in three months. Some mothers even drowned their babies from sheer desperation.[14]

The great spokesman against North American slavery, Frederick Douglass, captures the dehumanization involved from the moment of birth even when a newborn slave does manage to survive. He begins his renowned *Narrative of the Life of Frederick Douglass, an American Slave*, with a comment on his birth.

> I was born in Tuckahoe, near Hillsborough, and about twelve miles from Easton, in Talbot county, Maryland. I have no accurate knowledge of my age, never having seen any authentic record containing it. By far the larger part of the slaves know as little of their ages as horses know of theirs, and it is the wish of most masters within my knowledge to keep their slaves thus ignorant. I do not remember to have ever met a slave who could tell of his birthday.[15]

To reclaim birth is thus a revolutionary act in the context of slavery. It discloses hope for the newborn and the power to imagine a different future, one without bondage and tyranny; it means to reclaim subjecthood, to turn the birth of the oppressed into a meaningful event that needs to be recorded and narrated.

The story of the birth of ancient Israel is a story of trauma and recovery. The founding trauma in the nation's biography is bondage, the repression of growth. But then a process of recovery begins that entails the inversion of exposure from an antinatal act to a means of rescue. Yocheved casts her son into the Nile, but Moses' exposure is not meant to comply with Pharaoh's decree but rather to undo it. Similarly, the nation as a whole multiplies despite Pharaoh's tortuous measures and tireless attempts to restrict its growth: "But the more they afflicted them, the more they multiplied and grew" (Exod. 1:12). The relation between affliction and growth is provocatively inverted. While Pharaoh expected a reduction in the birthrate, his harsh treatment of the Hebrews led to the opposite, to a mysterious increase.

In Thy Blood Live

In his explicit and rather graphic use of the metaphor of birth vis-à-vis the nation, Ezekiel sheds much light on the representation of national formation in Exodus. In a famous passage in Ezekiel 16, which relates the story of national birth, Jerusalem stands for the nation:

> And as for thy nativity, in the day thou wast born thy navel was not cut, neither wast thou washed in water to supple thee; thou wast not salted at all, nor swaddled at all. None eye pitied thee, to do any of these unto thee, to have compassion upon thee, but thou wast cast out in the open field, to the lothing of thy person, in the day that thou wast born. And when I passed by thee, and saw thee polluted in thine own blood, I said unto thee when thou wast in thy blood, Live; yea, I said unto thee when thou wast in thy blood, Live. I

> have caused thee to multiply as the bud of the field, and thou hast increased and waxen great, and thou art come to excellent ornaments: thy breasts are fashioned, and thine hair is grown, whereas thou wast naked and bare. Now when I passed by thee, and looked upon thee, behold, thy time was the time of love; and I spread my skirt over thee, and covered thy nakedness. (4–8)

Israel was ruthlessly deserted by its parents at birth, soaking in blood helplessly without even receiving elementary postpartum care. The horrifying aspects of parental neglect are depicted in vivid detail. The newborn was not washed in water, her umbilical cord was not cut, her body was not salted (a practice that was apparently perceived as essential for the newborn's skin), nor was she swaddled. But then God passed by and adopted the neglected nation, adjuring Israel to live in her blood, to regard the marks of blood on her body as a source of life. What is more, He raised the nation and enabled her multiplication and growth. He provided her with the much-needed care and compassion that she lacked, washing the blood off her skin and furnishing her with excellent ornaments. Being a foundling nation is a traumatic experience, but it ultimately turns out to be beneficial: it leads (as is the case in the myth of the birth of the hero) to the discovery of / by more distinguished parents and ensures the transition from rags to riches, or rather from nakedness to royal garments.

The story of the Exodus is indeed the story of Israel's rescue and adoption by a more distinguished Father who is not merely royal but divine as well. It is a Father who has the force to wash off the signs of a collective trauma, to turn a helpless late-born nation into a powerful chosen one. In Ezekiel the adoption is construed as a marital bond between God and the nation, whereas in

Exodus it entails a bond between the Father and His firstborn son. In both cases the chosenness of Israel is defined in familial terms. The change in the representation of the nation's gender allows for a multifaceted treatment of the complex relation of Israel and God. Suffice it to say within the limited scope of this discussion that whereas the representation of the nation as female accentuates the erotic aspect in the relationship of God and the nation, the father-son dyad is far more concerned with questions of pedagogy and heroism.[16]

Revenge

Birth and revenge—or rather revenge fantasies—go hand in hand in Rank's analysis of birth myths. The hero's triumph over the "evil" father who tried to prevent his birth is a sign of utmost valor. A similar triumph may be traced in Exodus. Pharaoh, the antinatal force with respect to both Moses and the nation, is defeated, at first by the ongoing multiplication of the Hebrews and then in a direct confrontation: the ten plagues. Early commentators noted the gradual escalation of severity in the plagues beginning with nuisances and pests, continuing with destruction of livestock and crops, and ending with the gravest of all—the death of human beings.

This final plague seems to represent the final push in Israel's delivery. It is the night of Passover. Pharaoh, who has refused to set the Israelites free, suffers from a symmetrical punishment. The Egyptian firstborn die while God's firstborn, Israel, is saved. The differentiation between the Egyptians and the Hebrews is now enhanced by means of blood. God demands that the children of Israel take of the blood of the Paschal sacrifice and "strike it on the two side posts and on the upper door posts of the houses" so that it serve as "a token upon the houses where ye are: and when I see the blood, I will pass over you, and the plague shall not be upon you to destroy you, when I smite the land of Egypt" (Exod. 12:7–13).

The blood that marks the Israelites is not only apotropaic. Its location on the two side posts of the door evokes natal imagery.[17] The Israelites are delivered collectively out of the womb of Egypt. National birth, much like individual births (and all the more so in ancient times), takes place on a delicate border between life and death. It involves the transformation of blood from a signifier of death to a signifier of life. It also involves the successful opening of the womb, the prevention of the womb's turning into a tomb. The term "opener of the womb" (*peter rechem*) is introduced in Exodus 13:2 as a synonym for "firstborn." It appears in the depiction of the law regarding the firstborn, a law that is construed as a commemoration of the last plague: "And the Lord spake unto Moses, saying, Sanctify unto me all the firstborn, whatsoever openeth the womb among the children of Israel, both of man and of beast: it is mine." Although the term is not used explicitly with respect to the nation as a whole, this is precisely what is at stake in the context of the Exodus. The first opening of the womb (an act that is reminiscent of deflowering) is a unique and dangerous occurrence that requires divine vigilance. Those who do not deserve divine protection—namely, the Egyptians—find their death in the process, but Israel, God's firstborn, is consecrated as it opens the matrix.

Then comes the climactic moment of the delivery that includes the ultimate revenge: the scene by the Red Sea. Moses parts the waters at God's command. The Israelites walk on land in the midst of the sea, and the Egyptian soldiers, who are pursuing them, drown as the waters return. The downfall of the parent-nation seems total. Pharaoh, who wished to cast the Hebrew babies into the Nile, now finds his soldiers and fancy chariots sinking "like a stone" in the waters of the Red Sea.

"Did not old Pharaoh get lost, get lost, get lost in the Red Sea," marvels a famous African-American slave song. Lawrence Levine argues that the song promises that "power relations [are] not immutable" and conveys confidence in "the possibilities of instantaneous change."[18] Even if the scene by the Red Sea is something of a slave fantasy—there is no evidence in Egyptian sources of such a defeat, nor did the great Egypt disappear from the map at this time—the importance of the moment lies in its carnivalesque spirit, in the reversal of hierarchies. The master falls and the oppressed spring to life.

From now on, time will be perceived differently. Everything will be measured in relation to the moment in which God delivered Israel from Egypt. "This month shall be unto you the beginning of months: it shall be the first month of the year to you" (Exod. 12:2). A new calendar is established with the birth of the nation as its point of departure. It is a revolutionary moment that marks a wondrous new beginning.[19] Slavery is left behind, and the intoxicating smell of freedom is in the air.

Wonder

God performs a variety of wonders in Egypt (the ten plagues in fact are perceived as such), but the parting of the Red Sea seems to surpass them all. It marks the nation's first breath—out in the open air—and serves as a distinct reminder of the miraculous character of birth. Where there was nothing, a living creature emerges all of a sudden. If the myth of the birth of the hero accentuates the wonder of birth on an individual level, here the miracle is collective. Much like Moses, the nation is drawn out of the water against all odds. It is an intensified miracle: a wonder on a great scale. The two enormous walls of water, the ultimate breaking of the waters, and the exciting appearance of dry land all seem to represent a gigantic birth, a birth that is analogous to the creation of the world. The parting of the waters evokes Genesis 1, and the "blast" of God's "nostrils" on the waters (Exod. 15:8) calls to mind the creation of Adam in Genesis 2:7. "And the LORD God formed man of the dust of the ground, and breathed into his nostrils the breath of life." Accordingly, God is defined as the "maker" of the nation (*'am zu kanita*), a term that otherwise is used only in the context of the creation (Exod. 15:16).

On witnessing this great wonder, the people as a whole burst out singing. The Song of the Sea, with its fast tempo, celebrates the singularity of the nation's miraculous delivery. "Who is like unto thee, O Lord, among the gods? Who is like thee, glorious in holiness, fearful in praises, doing wonders? . . . For the horse of Pharaoh went in with his chariots and with his horsemen into the sea, and the Lord brought again the waters of the sea upon them; but the children of Israel went on dry land in the midst of the sea" (15:11–19). It is at once a breathtaking and breath-giving moment. All doubts and fears dissolve. Everything seems possible. Crossing the Red Sea is a leap of faith, a leap into life.

Martin Buber offers an insightful description of "The Wonder on the Sea" in *Moses*. He defines it as a moment of "abiding astonishment" that "no knowledge, no cognition, can weaken."

> The great turning-points in religious history are based on the fact that again and ever again an individual and a group ... wonder and keep on wondering; at a natural phenomenon, a historical event, or at both together. . . . Miracle is not something "supernatural" or "superhistorical," but an incident, an event which can be fully included in the objective, scientific nexus of nature and history; the vital meaning of which, however, for the person to whom it occurs, destroys the security of the whole nexus of knowledge for him, and explodes the fixity of the fields of experience named "Nature" and "History."[20]

The birth of the nation involves a bewildering blurring of the boundaries between nature and history. Nature participates in the shaping of this grand historical event, which is why the Song of the Sea is the Song of the Birth of the Nation. The sudden break in the rhythm of natural phenomena is used here to express the intense excitement of a nascent people.[21]

Divine Midwives

Much has been written on the image of God as Warrior in the Song of the Sea. Umberto Cassuto emphasizes the mythical dimension of God's victory over Pharaoh's host, pointing to other divine wars that hover in the background, above all, the crushing of the revolt of the sea by the Creator in the cosmic beginning.[22] He relies on Prophetic renditions of the parting of the Red Sea (e.g., Isa. 51:9–10) as well as on Mesopotamian texts such as the Babylonian creation myth, where Marduk overpowers Tiamat and then cuts her aquatic body into pieces.

The image of the Warrior is indeed a central image, but not the only one. God has feminine facets as well, though partially hidden.[23] Behind and against the "right hand" of the Warrior one can detect, I believe, a feminine hand: the strong magical hand of a grand Midwife drawing the newborn nation out of the depths of the sea, "the heart of the sea" (Exod. 15:8), into the world of the living, beyond the engulfing Flood. God, as it were, follows in the footsteps of the two midwives who loom so large in the opening chapter of Exodus, only here the Israelites need to be rescued from the "mighty waters" of the Red Sea rather than the Nile.[24] Ezekiel's depiction of the postpartum care that God bestows on the foundling nation reinforces the impression that the Father is something of a Midwife. The washing of the baby and the cutting of the umbilical cord were tasks usually performed by the midwife.[25] More important, they were at times, at least in Egyptian mythology, performed by divine midwives. A Middle Kingdom story records the miraculous birth of the first three kings of the Fifth Dynasty. The mother Rudjedet is attended at birth by the four goddesses Isis, Nephthys, Meskhenet, and Hekat. Each birth is represented in a similar manner:

> Isis placed herself before her [Rudjedet], Nephthys behind her, Hekat hastened the birth. Isis said: "Don't be so mighty in her womb, you whose name is 'Mighty.'" The child slid into her arms. . . . They washed him, having cut his navel cord, and laid him on a pillow of cloth. Then Meskhenet approached him and said: "A king who will assume the kingship in this whole land."[26]

In the Bible, however, the mythical delivery is not merely that of a king but of an entire nation that is treated as if it were royal.

That the Song of the Sea is sung by the women alone in the concluding lines of the scene adds yet another feminine touch to this miraculous birth. "And Miriam the prophetess, the sister of Aaron, took a timbrel in her hand; and all the women went out after her with timbrels and dances. And Miriam answered them, Sing ye to the Lord" (Exod. 15:20–21). Miriam, who stood between the reeds by the Nile watching over Moses' ark, orchestrating his deliverance, now dances by a Sea of Reeds (*yam suf*), with a timbrel in her hand, celebrating the redemption of the nation with an entire community of women.[27]

The Question of National Identity

The figuration of Israel's birth is a forceful unifying strategy, but the metaphor does not provide what Benedict Anderson calls "unisonance." Nations may try to fashion a coherent conception of identity, or origin, to seek unity at points of clear disjunction, but they are bound to fail. The intertwined biographies of Moses and Israel poignantly disclose the problematic of defining national identity both for the individual and for the community. Moses' birth story differs from that of his heroic counterparts at another point as well. He is transferred back and forth between his Hebrew and Egyptian mothers. Yocheved places him in a basket at the Nile; he is found by Pharaoh's daughter who then hands him back to Yocheved (believing her to be a wet nurse). Later Moses is brought back to the palace, where the princess adopts him and endows him with a name. He is raised in the palace but ultimately returns to his family and people.

The very fact that there are two sets of parents in the myth of the birth of the hero already intimates the difficulties involved in fashioning an identity. The myth addresses primary questions: Who am I? Who are my parents? Where do I come from? But the questions of origin become all the more complex when the two sets of parents pertain to two different nations. Moses' split national identity at birth will follow him for the rest of his life. When his first son is born in Midian he chooses to name him Gershom, saying, "I have been a stranger in a strange land" (Exod. 2:22). His naming speech relies on a pun that links the name "Gershom" with the word *stranger* (*ger*). But in what sense is Moses a stranger at this point—in relation to Midian (Jethro's daughters regard him as an Egyptian), or Egypt (his words echo the oracular announcement of Israel's troubling future as "a stranger [*ger*] in a land that is not theirs" in Gen. 15:13)?[28] Moses will devote most of his life to constructing the concept of Canaan as homeland and will lead his people persistently toward the land of "milk and honey," but ultimately he will die in the wilderness, between Egypt and the Promised Land.

And the nation? Israel's lineage is far more complicated than Moses' family tree, but here too the multiple parental figures point to diverse national origins. The conflict between God and Pharaoh is but one expression of the issue. The nebulous national identity of the two midwives is another case in point. Are the two midwives who deliver the Hebrew babies Egyptian or Hebrew? The problem stems from the indefinite use of "Hebrew" (*'ivriyot*) in Exodus 1:16. If it is to be read as an adjective, then Shiphrah and Puah are Hebrew midwives. But then there is another possibility. The verse may mean that these are Egyptian midwives who specialize in delivering Hebrew women. Numerous commentators have tried to solve the problem. Thus Josephus suggests that the king chose Egyptian midwives, assuming that they "were not likely to transgress his will." Similarly, Abarbanel claims that "they were not Hebrews but Egyptians, for how could he trust Hebrew women to put their own children to death." The midrash, however, perceived them as Hebrews and identified the two midwives with Yocheved and Miriam.[29] What these commentaries neglect to take into account is the significance of the indeterminate origin of the midwives, the extent to which the nation's story repeats the confusion about identity embedded in Moses' biography.

The children of Israel are torn between the two lands, between their deep ties to Egypt and their desire to seek another land. They were not raised in the Egyptian court, as Moses was, but nonetheless Egypt is not only the site of traumas for them: it served, however partially, as a nurturing motherland of sorts, especially the luscious land of Goshen. The birth of Israel entails a painful process of individuation from Egypt that is never fully resolved.[30] Just before the parting of the Red Sea, God promises the children of Israel that they shall see the Egyptians no more (Exod. 14:13). But the drowning of the Egyptians does not lead to the effacement of Israel's strong longings for the land of Egypt. National identity is thus poised on the brink of a "loss of identity."[31]

The Emergence of the National Voice: Internal Antinatal Forces

The nation's first words are delivered on the way out of Egypt, marking the rise of what Homi K. Bhabha calls "counter-narratives of the nation."[32] On seeing the Egyptian chariots pursuing them, the children of Israel cry out unto the Lord:

> And they said unto Moses, Because there were no graves in Egypt, hast thou taken us away to die in the wilderness? wherefore hast thou dealt thus with us, to carry us forth out of Egypt? Is not this the word that we did tell thee in Egypt, saying, Let us alone, that we may serve the Egyptians? For it had been better for us to serve the Egyptians, than that we should die in the wilderness? (Exod. 14:11–12)

National birth means gaining consciousness and the power of verbal expression. During their bondage in Egypt, the Israelites could only moan and groan. They were in a preverbal and preconscious state, unaware of God's providence. Or else their discourse was silenced (as they now claim), not deemed worthy of attention. Something changes with the Exodus. They acquire the capacity to verbalize their needs and cry out to the Lord through Moses. And yet the emergence of the voice of the nation is accompanied by antinatal cravings. They use their new power of expression to convey their discontent, their desire to return to Egypt, to undo the birth of the nation. In a fascinating way they question the official biography. God here turns out to be not the Deliverer of the nation but rather the bearer of death, an abusive Father who seeks to kill His children in the wilderness. God now seems to be just as bad as, or even worse than, Pharaoh.

The children of Israel are masters of complaint. This is just their first complaint, but it initiates a long series of murmurings in the desert. It has the characteristic rhetorical questions, much anguish, and anger. Nehama Leibowitz points to the obsessive evocation of the land they left behind in their grumbling. "'Egypt' is an eternal refrain in their mouths, recurring five times. They yearned for 'Egypt' as a babe for its mother's breasts."[33] Egypt seems to have far more to offer than the desert—even its graves (and Egypt does indeed excel in its death culture) are more attractive than those available in the wilderness. The primary national biography is far from linear. Birth does not necessarily move the children of Israel unambiguously forward. Another forceful desire compels them to look back toward Egypt.

Pharaoh, then, is not alone in wishing to stop the birth of the nation. Antinatal forces erupt from within as well. "The problem," as Bhabha claims, " is not simply the 'selfhood' of the nation as opposed to the otherness of other nations. We are confronted with the national split within itself, articulating the heterogeneity of the population."[34] Bhabha attributes such fractures to the disruptive power of minorities. The story of Israel is somewhat different. In this case, it is the *majority*—the vox populi—that questions the national presuppositions of the leading minority: Moses, his limited supporters—and God. The split is thus even more radical than in Bhabha's account of the modern nation, given its centrality. It stems from the conflicting desires of the bulk of the nation.

In a famous passage in "What Is a Nation?" Ernest Renan claims that "a nation's existence is, if you will pardon the metaphor, a daily plebiscite, just as an individual's existence is a perpetual affirmation of life."[35] For Renan, the nation is a spiritual principle, represented in the will to nationhood. It is this will that unifies a people, endowing them with a past, a future, and the lust for life. Renan, much like the biblical writers, cannot but rely on a personification of the nation in his exploration of nationhood. What the Bible adds to the picture, however, is an understanding of the complexity of national imagination; it reveals the extent to which the national affirmation of life may be accompanied by counterforces that do not see the formation of the nation as an urgent or essential project. A "daily plebiscite" in ancient Israel would have been a disaster. The children of Israel oscillate between a euphoric celebration of their deliverance—as is the case after the parting of the Red Sea—and a continual questioning of the official consecration of national birth.

Before the Israelites actually leave Egypt, Moses already turns the Exodus into a ritual to be cherished now and in days to come. He demands that they commemorate the event and pass the story on from one generation to another.

> And Moses said unto the people, Remember this day, in which ye came out from Egypt, out of the house of bondage; for by strength of hand the Lord brought you out from this place: there shall no leavened bread be eaten. . . . And thou shalt shew thy son in that day saying, This is done because of that which the Lord did unto me when I came forth out of Egypt. (Exod. 13:3–8)

Yerushalmi offers a fascinating analysis of the biblical injunction to remember the Exodus and the consequent ritualization of the event. What Yerushalmi overlooks is the extent to which the children of Israel cherish other memories as well. Against the recurrent command to remember the Exodus, they set up a countermemory: Egypt. Relentless, they persist in recalling life by the Nile, where they took pleasure in fleshpots and other Egyptian delights. Individuation from Egypt does not seem to be the only route. Memory can be shaped in a variety of ways.

Such counternarratives would seem to deflate national pride. Israel's heroism does not follow traditional perceptions of male courage. There is a good deal of fear of life in the nation's nascent voice and an acute horror of what lies ahead. God Himself often regrets having delivered the nation. The children of Israel do not succeed in fulfilling His expectations, and He never hesitates to express His disappointment in them. "You neglected the Rock that begot you, Forgot the God who brought you forth" (Deut. 32:18), claims Moses in God's name.[36] The people are blamed for being ungrateful, for forgetting even the unforgettable—the God who miraculously begot them. Of the numerous unflattering national designations God provides, the most resonant one is His definition of Israel as "a stiffnecked people" (Exod. 32:9). The nation withholds its body from God and in doing so reveals a sinful lack of faith and an unwillingness to open up to the divine Word.

But then Israel's challenge to the national plans of Moses and God is not merely a sign of weakness. There is something about the stiff neck of the nation and the refusal to take national imaginings for granted that reveals an unmistakable force. The nation's very name "Israel" means to struggle with God, and in a sense this is the nation's raison d'être. In this respect the biography of the eponymous father is also relevant to the understanding of national birth. Already in the womb Jacob struggles forcefully, trying to gain priority over his elder brother, Esau. Rebekah, who asks the Lord to explain the significance of the turmoil in her womb, is told, "Two nations are in thy womb, and two manners of people shall be separated from thy bowels; and the one people shall be stronger than the other people; and the elder shall serve the younger" (Gen. 25:23). We have seen the significance of the reversal of the primogeniture law on the national level, but what this primal scene equally emphasizes is the importance of the struggle for national formation. Not only the struggle with the other (Esau or Edom in this case) but also a struggle from within, a struggle with the Ultimate Precursor: God.[37] The uterine struggle between Jacob and Esau prefigures the momentous struggle with the angel. It is through wrestling in the night with a divine being that Jacob acquires the nation's name. "Thy name shall be called no more Jacob, but Israel," says the divine opponent, "for as a prince hast thou power with God and with men, and hast prevailed" (Gen. 32:28). Jacob does not become angelic as a result of this nocturnal encounter, but the struggle reveals a certain kind of intimacy with God that is unparalleled.

The nation, not unlike the eponymous father, is both the chosen son and the rebel son, and accordingly its relationship with the Father is at once intimate and strained. From the moment of Israel's birth, mutual adoration and disappointment mark the bond of the nation and God, and this is true of later stages in the nation's life as well. The tension between Israel and God only increases as the nation becomes a restless adolescent in the wilderness. In its rendition of the ambivalence that characterizes the father-son relationship, the primary biography of ancient Israel offers a penetrating representation of national ambivalence, making clear from the outset that the story of the nation is not a story without fissures and lapses.

The national biography of Israel surely relies on certain heroic motifs, but it does not omit unflattering moments in the nation's history. The representation of national birth in Exodus is not an idealized narrative about a flawless birth but rather a text that takes into account the darker aspects of national formation as it explores the baffling emergence of a new people. What makes nations come into being is one of the greatest enigmas that national biographies attempt to tackle. Exodus, I believe, can contribute much to our understanding of the imagining of such formative moments in its examination of how one nation jumped into the water despite itself and wondered why.

CHAPTER THREE

Suckling in the Wilderness

The Absent Mother

> Feeling the old horror come back—to want and want and not to have.
>
> *Virginia Woolf,* To the Lighthouse

> Here is no water but only rock
> Rock and no water and the sandy road
> The road winding above among the mountains
> Which are mountains of rock without water.
>
> *T. S. Eliot, "The Waste Land"*

The story of the journey in the desert is punctuated by recurrent statements that chart the various stations Israel passed through on the way from Egypt to the Promised Land: *vayis'u vayachanu*, "and they journeyed from . . . and encamped in." The names of the stations and the time spent in each one—measured in relation to the Exodus, the new calendar's point of departure—are recorded meticulously. A map of the nation's winding wanderings is drawn bit by bit. Yet we know very little about the character of the loci. The stations are almost indistinguishable topographically. There are no lengthy depictions of landscape, or of the heat of a merciless sun, or desert storms. Desert life entails but two central experiences: thirst and hunger.

The first attack of thirst takes place three days after the crossing of the Red Sea, in the desert of Shur. The climactic celebration of deliverance is replaced by an anxiety over water. Water is not to be found. Even when some water is detected in Mara, it is bitter and undrinkable. The people complain. "And the people murmured against Moses, saying, What shall we drink?" (Exod. 15:24). The least Moses could do after leading them to such a wasteland, their blunt and angry question seems to suggest, is to provide them with the most elementary substance of all: water. The name of the first stop, "Mara," the feminine form of the word *bitter*, imprints on the map of the desert the sense of acute thirst at the taste of bitter water. Shortly after, in the desert of Zin, "between Elim and Sinai, on the fifteenth day of the second month after their departing out of the land of Egypt," the assembly murmurs about hunger and accuses Moses of starving them to death, leading them astray to perish in the wilderness, far from the fullness of the savory fleshpots of Egypt. "Would to God we had died by the hand of the Lord in the Land of Egypt, when we sat by the flesh pots, and when we did eat bread to the full; for ye have brought us forth into this wilderness, to kill this whole assembly with hunger" (16:1–3). These are the first two incidents of thirst and hunger. Others will follow as the wanderings continue. Such stories bear witness to the harsh conditions of desert life, to the scarcity of water and food in arid and uninhabited zones. But their literal significance does not preclude their figurative implications. The voyage into the heart of the desert is a double voyage: both out there in a marked geographic space and within. And accordingly, the names of the stations, especially those invented along the road in commemoration of national scenes, often capture inner realities as they lay out the history of the nation's first reluctant steps.

Thirst and hunger, I would suggest, stand for a sharp and primary sense of loss. To be torn away from Egypt (a feminine noun —like all lands) seems to be analogous to the painful process of weaning, experienced by the infant at the disappearance of the overflowing breast of a nurturing mother.[1] The famous fleshpots of Egypt (*sir habasar*) represent, not merely an Egyptian delicatessen, but also the longed-for flesh of an absent mother. Left high and dry in the wilderness, without the mother's body, without her sweet milk (the very antithesis of bitter water), the children of Israel fear total annihilation. Deserted at birth, they now feel deserted once again in an unbearable exile. The wandering Israelites cry much as the exiles who sat by the rivers of Babylon cried on remembering Zion (Ps. 137:1), only their notion of motherland does not coincide with the official one. Egypt is the land they mourn over, the land of their dreams, not Zion.

The metaphor of national suckling is explicitly dealt with in Numbers 11, at another site of complaint. On this occasion the people once again crave the food they thrived on back in Egypt. Moses, who is quite a complainer himself, turns to God and asks:

> Have I conceived all this people? have I begotten them, that thou shouldest say unto me, Carry them in thy bosom, as a

nursing father beareth the sucking child, unto the land which thou swarest unto their fathers? (11:12)

The wandering nation in the wilderness is likened to a vulnerable suckling (*yonek*) who needs to be nursed and carried in the bosom in order to survive. In ancient times breast feeding was regarded as an indispensable gift of life. Without a nursing mother or a wet nurse, an infant had little or no chance of survival. The dangers of infancy were numerous and child mortality high. A whole range of spells and amulets from the ancient Near East disclose the anxieties involved in rearing a child. Thus Egyptian papyri from the early New Kingdom include a spell for the mother's milk, meant to assure its flow and quality. And given the tremendous dependence on the supply of milk, wet nurses acquired high status in the Egyptian royal court and in the households of elite families.[2] Something of this tradition is evident in Genesis 35:8, where the burial of Deborah, Rebekah's wet nurse, under "the oak of weeping" beneath Bethel (a site of worship?), is deemed worthy of recording.[3]

Phyllis Trible quotes Numbers 11:12 in her groundbreaking work, *God and the Rhetoric of Sexuality*, to corroborate her notion that God has feminine facets that are no less important than His male traits.[4] She fails to see, however, that God is more often than not represented as male in the Bible and that in this case His maternal capacities are called into question. Moses' rhetorical questions imply that God, who begot the nation and thus is responsible for its well-being, has not been very successful in fulfilling the "child's" needs. And if He has not managed to provide the children of Israel with the much-needed maternal nurturing, why should Moses be capable of assuming the role of the nation's nurse (*'omen*)?[5] Conceiving a people is not the end of the story. In dreams begin responsibilities. After national birth comes the challenging task of fashioning the breasts that would sustain a people and the bosom that would provide the essential warmth and support throughout the long and turbulent journey to the Promised Land.

The work of Melanie Klein may be illuminating in probing into the significance of the metaphor of suckling in the biblical text. For Klein, the earliest relation of the infant to the body of the nursing mother generates the central drama in the psyche of the infant. "The mother's milk," she writes, "which first stills the baby's pangs of hunger and is given to him by the breast which he comes to love more and more, acquires for him emotional value which cannot be overrated. The breast and its product, which first gratify his self-preservative instinct as well as his sexual desires, come to stand in his mind for love, pleasure and security."[6] The intense gratification at the mother's breast reinforces an idealization that experience tends to frustrate. The child senses the mother's nurturance as insufficient at times and resents her control over it. The breast releases milk in limited quantities and then disappears. Rage at the evasive breast intermingles with fear and anxiety. When the breast is wanted and is not to be found, the infant feels that it is lost forever along with the mother. "The actual experience of weaning greatly reinforces these painful feelings or tends to substantiate these fears; but in so far as the baby never has uninterrupted possession of the breast, and over and over again is in the state of lacking it, one could say that, in a sense, he is in a constant state of being weaned or at least in a state leading up to weaning."[7] Weaning turns out to be the prototype of mourning, a process through which the infant first experiences loss and comes to terms with it.[8]

Moses' provocative questions may be seen as a comment on suckling and its discontents, on the impossibility of fulfilling even the needs of an individual baby, let alone a nursing nation. They may also imply that a predominantly male God has even less of a chance to produce the required amount of milk. The image of Egypt, the bountiful motherland, cannot so easily be forgotten and replaced. Her loss parches the people's throats and gives rise to intense and painful longings for the life-sustaining maternal gift that was, as it were, stolen from them, gone forever.

The Bible complicates the primary drama of suckling and weaning not only by introducing a Father who plays the role of a mother but also by dealing with the respective perspectives of both the child and the parent (Klein, as some of her critics note, focuses on the former).[9] While the children of Israel are continuously disappointed by God's lack of nurturing, God scolds the grumbling nation for its lack of faith and its insatiability. Anger goes both ways, and "testing" or "trying" too. God tests Israel's capacity to keep His commandments through water and food, and the nation, in its turn, tests God's vigilance and love. Indeed, the same root, *nsh*, is used in both cases. A closer look at the construction of national thirst and hunger is necessary to better understand the shaping of this drama in the biography of ancient Israel.

Thirst: Rocks and Rods

The two major scenes of thirst, in Exodus 17 and Numbers 20, recount the striking of rocks with rods in quest of water. The relation of such scenes to suckling becomes clear in the Song of Moses, where God is praised for enabling the nation to "suck honey out of the rock" (Deut. 32:13). In Exodus and Numbers, however, "sucking" out of rocks is not as ideal or sweet. These are moments of intense conflict, so much so that the station where the first incident takes place is called Massah and Meribah (literally, trial and quarrel) and the water of the second episode is defined as "water of quarrel," *mey meriva.* Let us begin with the earlier quarrel.

> And there was no water for the people to drink. Wherefore the people did chide with Moses, and said, Give us water that we may drink. And Moses said unto them, Why chide ye with me? wherefore do ye tempt the Lord? And the people thirsted there for water; and the people murmured against Moses, and said, Wherefore is this that thou hast brought us up out of Egypt, to kill us and our children and our cattle with thirst? And Moses cried unto the Lord, saying, What shall I do unto this people? they be almost ready to stone me. And the Lord said unto Moses, Go on before the people, and take with thee of the elders of Israel; and thy rod, wherewith thou smotest the river, take in thine hand, and go. Behold, I will stand before thee there upon the rock in Horeb; and thou shalt smite the rock, and there shall come water out of it, that the people may drink. And Moses did so in the sight of the elders of Israel. (Exod. 17:1–6)

The people are desperate. "Give us water," they demand of Moses (and Aaron presumably), implying that they have supplies of water but are withholding them mercilessly. And when Moses rebukes them for their demands, which he interprets as a trial of God, they blame him for bringing them out of Egypt only to kill them and their cattle by thirst. The people come close to stoning Moses—or so he claims. Double murder is at stake. The people regard Moses (and God by extension) as a murderer, whereas Moses depicts the people as a lynch mob. Moses is not literally murdered (contra Freud), nor are the people, but such fantasies are in the air. God finally intervenes and introduces the possibility of striking rocks instead of stoning people. Violence does not dissipate; it is now regulated by the magical rod. Moses, we are reminded, struck with the rod before, back in Egypt, when the Nile turned red with blood. It is not accidental that this particular stroke of the rod is mentioned. Here too the question revolves around water (and blood) and the desire to gain control over its sources.[10]

Moses mediates between God and the community. As a leader, he is more of a parent than a child, but then he is human, which means that he has much in common with the people. In striking the rock with his rod, Moses in a sense is more the people's agent than God's. He gives expression to their acute desire to seize God's hidden waters. "Rock" (*tsur*), after all, is one of God's names—and this particular rock is all the more associated with Him for it is the rock of Horev, where He first revealed Himself to Moses and later to the community as a whole.[11] The divine title "Rock" is usually understood as a metaphor for God's force and stability. In this connection it also attests to the difficulties embedded in suckling from a God whose breasts are as hard as rocks and whose milk needs to be drawn out by force. God's body is as stiff as the nation's neck.

The story ends with an etiological remark about the name of the place. It is called Massah and Meribah, we are told, because of the quarrel (*riv*) of the children of Israel, "and because they tempted [tested, *nasotam*] the Lord, saying, Is the Lord among us, or not?" (Exod. 17:7). The people are enraged at God's absence at a moment when He is needed so badly. Lack of water is regarded as a sign of abandonment. What they are expected to learn from the incident is that even dry rocks can miraculously produce fresh water and that God is present and loving even when he seems to be absent. But the question of divine presence remains provocatively open as it lurks behind the name of this site.

The second scene of rod and rocks takes place toward the end of the journey, at Kadesh. The repetition may seem monotonous at first but is not without significance; it creates a rhythm of a whining child and matches the slow and frustrating pace of a voyage whose end recedes time and again.[12] Each complaint story, however, has its own makeup. There are certain differences between Massah and Meribah and the striking of the rock at Kadesh that point to an escalation of the conflict in the course of the wanderings.

> And there was no water for the congregation: And they gathered themselves together against Moses and against Aaron. And the people chode with Moses, and spake, saying, Would God that we had died when our brethren died before the Lord! . . . And wherefore have ye made us to come up out of Egypt, to bring us in unto this evil place? it is no place of seed . . . neither is there any water to drink. . . . And the Lord spake unto Moses, saying, Take the rod, and gather thou the assembly together, thou, and Aaron thy brother, and speak ye unto the rock before their eyes; and it shall give forth his water, and thou shalt bring forth to them water out of the rock. . . . And Moses and Aaron gathered the congregation

> together before the rock, and he said unto them, Hear now, ye rebels; must we fetch you water out of this rock? And Moses lifted up his hand, and with his rod he smote the rock twice: and the water came out abundantly. . . . And the Lord spake unto Moses and Aaron, Because ye believed me not, to sanctify me in the eyes of the children of Israel, therefore ye shall not bring this congregation into the land which I have given them. This is the water of Meribah [quarrel]; because the children of Israel strove with the Lord, and he was sanctified in them. (Num. 20:2–13)

The people grumble as usual, wishing they were back in Egypt, though their complaint now is more elaborate in its depiction of the futility and utter desolation of the desert. What is more, death in the wilderness is no longer mere fantasy. They wish to share the fate of their dead brothers, whom God had killed earlier along the road (the spies, Korah and his congregation, to mention but a few). Their death wish is a sarcastic remark about the heavy cost and futility of national endeavors. Under such circumstances, under such severe thirst, they seem to claim, one can hardly imagine national growth.

Moses loses his temper. He calls the people rebels, then strikes the rock instead of speaking to it as God had commanded. Worse, he strikes the rock twice. Is this why he is punished so severely? Indeed, many commentators trace disbelief in his impatience (e.g., Rashi, Rambam, Shadal). Others have suggested that Moses' conduct comes close to magic. Moses seems to assume the role of a magician in regarding himself and Aaron as those who have the power to bring forth water (20:10), failing to consecrate the divine hand that made the miracle possible.[13] By using the rod—a traditional tool of the magician—when it was not necessary, Moses further discloses his reliance on magic rather than on God.[14] The text does not yield a clear-cut solution to the riddle of what made God's wrath kindle, but situating this scene within the national drama of suckling and weaning may shed some light on the matter. The angry response of God in this case, I believe, foregrounds the darker facets of suckling out of rocks as it lays bare what is only implicit in Exodus 17: the violent and impious impulses that such striking entails. Striking rocks verges on blasphemy insofar as it implies a struggle with God, a vehement and relentless knocking on His hard, unyielding body. The punishment meted out to Moses and Aaron—death in exile—is modeled on the "sin." Doubting God's capacity to produce water, they are doomed to remain forever in the arid land of the desert, like the rest of their generation.

Manna and Meat

The word *manna* captures the wonder evoked by its appearance in the midst of the wilderness. "Man hu"—What is it? ask the people on seeing the soft flakes of manna covering the "face of the wilderness," mingled with a layer of morning dew (Exod. 16:13–15). The manna is described in poetic language that underlines its miraculous and divine character. God promises to "rain bread from heaven" in response to the people's demand for food (16:4). It is not conventional bread whose source is the earth but rather heavenly bread that comes from above, like rain. The manna is more a liquid than dry food, alleviating both thirst and hunger. The taste of it is exquisite—"like wafers made with honey" (16:31) or rich cream, *leshad hashemen* (Num. 11:8)—and its color white as coriander seed.[15] What is it but heavenly, sweet, creamy milk that allows the entire congregation to nurse at once.

Manna drops from heaven with a primary set of laws, allowing God to "test" the people (*lema'an anasenu*) and see "whether they will walk in [His] law, or no" (Exod. 16:4). Every man is expected to gather manna "according to his eating" (16:18) and leave none until morning. Food is to be distributed justly, so that however much one gathered, it wondrously amounted to one *'omer*.[16] Everyone was worthy of eating manna to the full. But with the Law comes its violation. Some members of the community disobey Moses and keep the gathered manna until the next morning. The manna "bred worms, and stank" (16:20), losing its nu-minous life-giving qualities, becoming susceptible to the deadly forces of decay. More violations follow as the people ignore Moses' instructions and set out to gather manna on the Sabbath. "How long refuse ye to keep my commandments and my laws?" (16:28) asks God, enraged by the excruciatingly slow nature of pedagogical undertakings. The voyage is as long on the parental side.

National pedagogy requires a consideration of future generations as well.

> And Moses said, This is the thing which the Lord commandeth, Fill an omer of it to be kept for your generations; that they may see the bread wherewith I have fed you in the wilderness, when I brought you forth from the land of Egypt. And Moses said unto Aaron, Take a pot, and put an omer full of manna therein, and lay it up before the Lord, to be kept for your generations. . . . And the children of Israel did eat manna forty years, until they came to a land inhabited; they did eat manna, until they came unto the borders of the land of Canaan. (16:32–35)

Moses insists on the preservation of the substance itself, by the ark, as tangible testimony for days to come. Interestingly, the manna is put in a pot that seems to serve as the counterpart of the Egyptian fleshpots. The term for the manna pot, *tsintsenet*, is a unique term (used only in this context) that highlights the unparalleled quality of God's food. The fragility of collective memory, however, is evident in the following break in chronological sequence. A poetic note is inserted for those who have not heard the story of the manna and do not know that the people were fed by heavenly bread until they reached the borders of the Promised Land.[17]

The second story of manna is a more violent one. Here, as in the case of the rock and rod stories, the repetition of the story in Numbers entails an intensification of the quarrel. The nation is older, as it were, and accordingly its nutritional expectations are higher.

> And the children of Israel also wept again, and said, Who shall give us flesh to eat? We remember the fish, which we did eat in Egypt freely; the cucumbers, and the melons, and the leeks, and the onions, and the garlic: But now our soul is dried away: there is nothing at all, beside this manna, before our eyes. (Num. 11:4–6)

As their appetite grows, the memory of Egypt becomes more fanciful and appetizing. The trauma of slavery, still evident in the first complaint on the bank of the Red Sea (Exod. 14:12), is forgotten once Egypt fades below the horizon. The farther they go into the wilderness, the only "real" hardships seem to be those of desert life. Out of such oblivions spring tales. Egypt's fleshpots now include an abundance of fish, juicy vegetables, and spices.

What the people remember, however, is not entirely groundless. They bring to the fore earlier, sweeter memories of a benevolent Egypt, whose fertile land rescued the patriarchs way back, when famine struck Canaan, and then enabled the initial growth of the nation.[18]

Against this rich culinary Egyptian background, the manna seems terribly pale. Instead of quenching thirst and alleviating hunger, it turns out to be a source of dryness, "drying away" not quite their "soul," as the King James Version has it, but rather their "lives" (*nefesh*). It invades their world from all sides, shriveling up their surroundings, leaving room for nothing else before their eyes. The official parental line defines manna as a divine gift of unsurpassable value and taste, but the people, at this point, perceive it as the very opposite. It is more of a punishment than a gift, and, above all, it lacks the power to replace Egypt. They starve for more substantial food that would delight both their eyes and their stomachs, adding color to the dull diet of the desert. They want flesh, not manna.

This is where Moses' complaint about God's limited nursing powers appears. Exhausted by the heavy burden of the ceaseless demands of the people, he passes on the responsibility for their care to their Father. God accepts the challenge and assures the crying people that there will be meat; in fact, more than enough. "Ye shall not eat one day, nor two days, nor five days, neither ten days, nor twenty days; But even a whole month, until it came out of your nostrils" (Num. 11:19–20). They don't like His food—which means, as every mother knows, that they don't like Him. He'll show them the wonders He can cook up. They'll have more and better food than they ever dreamed of having. Despite God's promise, Moses cannot imagine finding in the desert sufficient food to satisfy the needs of six thousand people. "Shall the flocks and the herds be slain for them, to suffice them? or shall all the fish of the sea be gathered together for them, to suffice them?" (Num 11:22). The superlative character of his questions indicates that the desert is no place for extravagant promises, but it also suggests that even if all the fish of the sea and the flocks of the mountains were gathered together, they would not suffice to fulfill the insatiable desires of an ungrateful people. The meat finally comes from the one species Moses did not evoke: birds. But before the quail is delivered, Moses needs to learn a lesson about the distribution of authority. He is not exempt from education.

Food and government are inextricably connected. The people are not simply "pedagogical objects," to use Bhabha's terms, they have a role in the fashioning of law and leadership.[19] The grumbling of the people leads to a different configuration of power as it spurs Moses to better manage the provision of food. Seventy elders are gathered, and the spirit that God "put" on Moses is transferred onto them so that "they shall bear the burden of the people" (Num. 11:17). Others, Eldad and Medad, are touched by the spirit of God and begin to prophesy in the camp without the mediation of Moses. To carry an entire nation one needs more than one bosom.

The quail is presented as a new item in the national diet, although it is already mentioned briefly in Exodus 17. The descent of flesh is as poetic as that of manna. God can "rain" birds, not only bread. A wind of God (the term used is *ruach,* the very term that earlier depicted the emanation of God's spirit from Moses to the elders) blows from the sea, carrying with it quail, gently strewing them around the camp, with much care, so that they land exactly within reach, but a day's journey on each side and no more than "two cubits high upon the face of the earth" (Num. 11:31; see also Ps. 78:26–31). God moves heaven and earth to fetch the people the flesh they crave, but once again there is a question regarding quantity and limits.

Excited by the sudden appearance of meat, some people gather quail with no sense of limit. Hunger, they suspect, may return at any moment. They gather all day, and then during the night, and the next day as well. Ten omers at least per person. God's response is extreme. Mercilessly, He snatches their lives away, "while the flesh was yet between their teeth" (Num. 11:33), before it was even chewed. Gluttonous cravings are regarded as an unforgivable transgression, an expression of forbidden lust. The wilderness includes, at times, harsh pedagogical practices.[20] Even when food is given one cannot be certain that it will be digested. Death may cut off one's life in the midst of a bite. Here as before the violent incident leaves a mark on the map, for a new name is invented: "And he called the name of that place Kibroth hattaavah [the tombs of lust]: because there they buried the people that lusted" (11:34). In Deuteronomy God actually admits that he starved the nation in the wilderness, subjecting it to numerous hardships. He did so, however, for a reason—much as a loving father disciplines his son (Deut. 8:3–6). This is a more normative account of what takes place in Exodus and Numbers, where the Father's violence seems somewhat excessive and inexplicable: love, lust, jealousy, and rage intersect in unpredictable ways.

In an article entitled "Exodus," Benedict Anderson speaks of exile—whether literal or figurative—as the "nursery of nationality," the condition that gives rise to the acts of imagination necessary for the construction of nationhood.[21] Anderson says nothing about biblical Israel, but his title suggests that the story of the

Exodus encapsulates the intricacies of national formation. Such "nurseries," however, are never that peaceful. The complaint scenes in the wilderness lay bare the violence and difficulties that are part and parcel of the shaping of ancient Israel. The character and future of the newborn nation are negotiated among the people, Moses, and God through complaining (they all complain in one way or another) and testing. To determine the national diet means to determine, among other things, the nature of government as well as the cultural bent of the nation.

The Nursing Goddess and Monotheistic Censorship

When the people long to return to Egypt, they do not merely long for "flesh." Exile entails an agonizing uprooting from a cultural setting and the loss of familiar customs and codes. In the thirst and hunger of the wandering Israelites one can trace religious longings of a forbidden sort, a craving for "strange milk." Egyptian religion was by no means matriarchal (the Egyptian pantheon, like other polytheistic pantheons, was run by supreme male deities), but it had a series of alluring mother goddesses, one of the prominent ones being Isis. Isis, also known as the "lady of enchantments," gained renown for her successful resurrection of her husband-brother, Osiris, and later for saving her son, Horus. She raised her newborn son in secret, hiding him in the papyrus marshes, to protect him from the evil designs of Seth (his uncle). This close guarding of Horus from danger became a frequent point of reference in magical texts concerning cures for children's ailments.[22] One of the most popular images of Isis (both in drawings and in statuettes) was the image of a suckling goddess, expressing milk from her breast, with Horus sitting on her lap.[23]

In the Pyramid Texts, the king is depicted as the living embodiment of Horus, sustained by Isis's divine milk. In other contexts she is defined as the royal wet nurse. In either case, she is regarded as the protecting and nourishing goddess whose milk is crucial to the growth of the king. Goddesses—not only in Egyptian culture—caress kings and heroes in their bosoms and offer their breasts to them. The myth of the birth of the hero develops into the myth of the suckling hero. Rank attributed the nursing of heroes to "lowly" women, or animals, the most prominent example being the suckling of Remus and Romulus by the she-wolf. More often than not, however, milk comes from above in mythological contexts, infused with divine qualities, a curious combination of material and spiritual sustenance that assures the special status of the suckling hero and occasionally grants him a touch of immortality (Hercules, who manages to draw a few drops from Hera's breast, is one such case).[24]

The Bible fashions a different myth, a myth of a nursing Father who brings forth water out of rocks and drops manna and quail from the sky—not merely for an individual hero but for an entire community. It is, however, a God whose work is revealed in history, which means that myth is set against the disorderly character of historical events and the facts of life, such as frustration and death, thirst and hunger. The complex interweaving of myth and history had much to offer but could not preclude longings for a cultural past in which suckling was provided by a more tender Mother, unambiguously female. The separation from the well-established religion of Egypt was not a simple task, nor was there national accord as to the preferable mode of individuation. The heavy reliance of Roman culture on Greek traditions points to another possible route for fashioning a new cultural identity vis-à-vis a powerful precursor.[25] Monotheism, however, required a clear-cut break with other cultures and was willing to admit no debt to earlier sources.

Despite the harshness of monotheistic censorship, the people oppose the Mosaic demand to eradicate the heritage of Egypt and attempt to maintain a few drops of milk from their lost cultural past. When the children of Israel actually give more concrete expression to their repressed desires, they forge a golden calf—not a nursing goddess. But where there is a calf, there must have been a cow.

In *Moses and Monotheism,* Freud offers an intriguing account of biblical censorship in his attempt to uncover the murder of Moses by the wandering Israelites.

> The distortion of a text is not unlike a murder. The difficulty lies not in the execution of the deed but in doing away with the traces. One could wish to give the word "distortion" the double meaning to which it has a right, although it is no longer used in this sense. It should mean not only "to change the appearance of," but also "to wrench apart," "to put in another place." That is why in so many textual distortions we may count on finding the suppressed and abnegated material hidden away somewhere, though in an altered shape and torn out of its original connection. Only it is not always easy to recognize it.[26]

Although Freud was not interested in the traces of the mother goddess in the wilderness (this is the one perfect murder he attributes to Judaism), his analysis of the dynamics of repression is most appropriate in this respect. The Calf, I would conjecture, is a distorted and displaced image of Isis. It is a suckling calf that speaks of the absence of a suckling cow. Isis, one should bear in mind, was represented at times in the shape of a cow or in human form, wearing a cow-horn crown. Some scholars assume that the Golden Calf stands for Apis, the sacred bull of Egyptian religion, but given the fact that what we have here is a calf—not a bull—it is more plausible to see Isis as the primary reference.[27] That Moses grinds the Golden Calf and makes the congregation drink its dust with water reinforces the notion that suckling and weaning are at stake. Moses tries to wean the nation from its yearnings for idolatrous water by drawing a distinction between pure sources and muddy waters, or in Jeremiah's terms, between seeking the "Fount of living water" and "going to Egypt to drink the waters of the Nile" (Jer. 2:13–18).[28]

As I suggested elsewhere, Isis may also be traced, in modified form, in the female figures of the Exodus.[29] Her role of deliverer-nurse-mother-sister-wife is "wrenched apart" as it is divided among the two midwives, Yocheved, Pharaoh's daughter, Miriam, and Zipporah. In the context of the suckling Isis, the most conspicuous parallel is Yocheved. Yocheved nurses Moses against all odds. Moses, who is torn off his mother's breasts when he is put in the basket, among the bulrushes, returns to her bosom unexpectedly. Miriam, as one recalls, tricks Pharaoh's daughter into hiring Yocheved as a wet nurse for her own son. Like Horus, Moses manages to benefit from maternal protection and nurturance despite his persecutors. He is endowed with a double gift of life: first at birth and then in the vulnerable period of infancy. Yocheved's milk loses something of the divine character of Isis's milk, given that she is a mere mortal, but it acquires instead tremendous historical and national value, which is why such an effort is made to preserve it: this is the milk Moses needs to suck in order to return to his people later on and deliver them; it provides the primary national marking and a lesson about the ways in which Pharaoh's edict may be resisted.

Rise Up, O Well

The dryness of the desert attests to different kinds of maternal absence not only in the heavenly sphere but also in the earthly one. The biography of ancient Israel allots strikingly little space for maternal figures in the wilderness. Once the children of Israel leave Egypt behind, the women who took part in the initial stages of the revolution practically disappear. The two midwives vanish; Yocheved is mentioned again only in genealogies (Exod. 6:20; Num. 26:59), and Zipporah is sent off after delivering Moses from God's wrath at the strange night of "The Bridegroom of Blood" (Exod. 4).

Even Miriam who, more than the others, acquires a visible role on the national stage through her leading of the women in song and dance after the crossing of the Red Sea is struck with leprosy for criticizing Moses' exclusive position and demanding that her prophetic powers be acknowledged (Num. 12).[30] Miriam dies shortly after being shut out of the camp on account of leprosy and is buried in Kadesh. Her death is recorded in a brief statement that is immediately followed by the story of the "water of quarrel": "And the people abode in Kadesh; and Miriam died there, and was buried there. And there was no water for the congregation" (Num. 20:1–2). A noticeable omission lurks between the two verses. No national mourning over her death is mentioned, in contradistinction to the burial scenes of both Aaron and Moses. Are the tears shed over lack of water the missing tears of mourning?[31] Put differently, does Miriam's death intensify the thirst in the dry palates of the people as it triggers the memory of Egypt's lost fleshpots (mourning piling up on mourning)? Does the severity of the quarrel over water in this site have something to do with Miriam's death? Is the sanctity of Kadesh (the name is a derivation of the word *holy*) related to the fact that Miriam was buried there?

The midrash aptly captured Miriam's special relationship to water in attributing to her a wandering well. The well appears in the midrashic interpretation of Micah 6:4, where Moses, Aaron, and Miriam are listed as the three leaders who brought Israel out of Egypt. The merit of the three deliverers, claims the midrash, ensured that the nation receive various gifts throughout the wanderings in the desert.

> The well was due to the merit of Miriam, who sang by the waters of the Red Sea: *And Miriam sang (wa-ta'an) unto them: Sing ye to the Lord* (Ex. xv, 21), *and by the waters of the well, Then sang Israel this song, Rise Up, O well, sing (enu) ye unto it* (Num. xxi, 17). . . . How was the well constructed? It was rock-shaped like a kind of bee-hive, and wherever they journeyed it rolled along and came with them. (Bamidbar Rabbah I, 2)

The midrash adheres strictly to proof texts and at the same time provides extravagant supplements. If the well is attributed to Miriam, it is because her singing at the Red Sea resonates in the collective singing by the well in Numbers 21:17. The rabbis rely on the similarity between the two occasions and above all on the recurrent use of the root *'anh*—a rare term for singing—in the context of water. The fact that Miriam is already dead in

Numbers 21 does not deter them from reaching this conclusion. On the contrary, the call of the people for the well to "rise up" is seen as proof that after Miriam dies, the well disappears and needs to be restored. The well is "rock-shaped," with many holes like a beehive; it offers an image of a sweet rock (there must be honey in this beehive) that seems more accessible and present than God's Rock; it also provides the missing maternal counterpart to the pillars of cloud and fire.

A Land of Milk and Honey

The need for a more pronounced maternal image in the national imagination, however, did not escape the biblical writers. The biography of ancient Israel does put forth one legitimate mother on the national map: the Promised Land, the land that "floweth with milk and honey."[32] Much has been written about the plenitude conveyed by this expression, but little attention has been given to the choice of milk and honey in particular, that is, to the implied maternal facets of the representation of the land. The word *floweth*, *zavat*, is usually used in the context of bodily fluids, reinforcing the notion that the land is a maternal body, with admirable flowing breasts.[33] From the very beginning in Egypt (Exod. 13:5), Moses and God fashion an infantile dream of wish fulfillment, a land where milk is always available, flowing in abundance, intermingled with honey. In the wilderness the Israelites receive but a partial introduction to these maternal treasures, but in Canaan, presumably, the ultimate pleasure awaits them.

Israel's weaning is terminable and interminable—in part because of the confusing character of the monotheistic God who insists on playing contradictory roles at once. As a patriarchal Father, He is eager to wean the suckling child and to speed up Israel's separation from the maternal fleshpots of Egypt. At the same time God wants to be the ultimate Mother, a Mother whose sweet milk is far superior to that of Egypt, whether it is provided via manna and rocks in the wilderness or via the land, later on in Canaan. The interminability of weaning, however, is also an insightful comment on the ways in which infantile fantasies linger on beyond infancy. I began with the aspects of weaning that are embedded in suckling, the frustrations at an evasive breast, but the opposite is true as well. The desire to suckle and the acute longings for a lost maternal paradise do not disappear with weaning: they still resonate at later stages of one's life.

The Promised Land is imagined as a perfect mother with a perfect nature who can satisfy all the desires of the young nation: plenitude, pleasure, love, and security. The paradisiacal qualities of the locus are elaborated in Isaiah's vision of Jerusalem as the utopian mother:[34]

> Rejoice ye with Jerusalem, and be glad with her . . . that you may suck, and be satisfied with the breasts of her consolations; that you may milk out, and be delighted with the abundance of her glory. For thus saith the Lord, Behold, I will extend peace to her like a river . . . then shall ye suck, ye shall be borne upon her sides, and be dandled upon her knees. As one whom his mother comforteth, so will I comfort you. (66:10–13)

Way out there beyond the desert there is an alternative motherland, far better than Egypt, the official line argues. But while the Israelites wander in the wilderness, oscillating between thirst and hunger, Egypt seems far more tangible. And then, as we shall see, even when Canaan is finally approached, in the story of the spies (Num. 13), the image of utopian suckling falls apart in an uncanny way. Canaan, much like Egypt, is far from being a perfect motherland on closer inspection.

Inscriptions in the Desert

Later traditions turn the desert itself into a longed-for site. Jeremiah recalls nostalgically the days of Israel's "youth" in the wilderness (2:2), and Hosea dreams of a day in which God will allure Israel and bring the nation back to the wilderness to renew the covenant (2:14). These are, no doubt, idealizations of the wandering period, but they are not inattentive to the complexities of its representation in the Pentateuch.[35] Exile is no paradise. And yet the greatest revelation of all takes place on Mount Sinai—not in the Promised Land.[36] For behind the complaints, the thirst, and the hunger that characterize the wanderings in the desert, there is life, a yearning to fill the "howling waste" (Deut. 32:10) of the desert with marks.

Moses and Monotheism, as Michel de Certeau has taught us, takes into account the loss and mourning at the base of historiographical writing. Freud attributes to Moses' death a central role in the nation's history and sees the initial "drowning" of monotheistic religion (like Schiller's song) as the condition that promised its powerful return.[37] What de Certeau and Freud overlook is the more primary loss and mourning that shape biblical historiography: the exile from Egypt and the repression of the Mother. It is this loss that gives rise to the desire to sing to a well, to turn bare rocks into tablets with inscriptions, and to fashion out of a desolate labyrinthian inscape a map.

CHAPTER FOUR

At the Foot of Mount Sinai

National Rites of Initiation

Thus shalt thou say to the house of Jacob,
and tell the children of Israel;
Ye have seen what I did unto the Egyptians,
and how I bare you on eagles' wings,
and brought you unto myself.
Now therefore, if ye will obey my voice indeed,
and keep my convenant,
then ye shall be a peculiar treasure unto me
above all people:
for all the earth is mine:
And ye shall be unto me a kingdom of priests,
and an holy nation.

Exod. 19:3–6

So proclaims God in the initial ceremonial address to the people at Mount Sinai. It is a climactic point in the biography of ancient Israel, the opening note of the momentous initiation rites of Sinai.

The diction ascends above the level of prose and assumes poetic form, as befits a passage dealing with such an exalted topic.[1] Before the law, before the smoke, the fire, the thunder, and the cloud, comes poetry. The beautiful image of the "eagles' wings" likens the journey up the mountain to an exhilarating swift, smooth flight beyond the dangers and the dreariness of the human world below. The agony of slavery as well as the miseries of thirst and hunger along the road vanish for a while. On bringing the people to His mountain, God lures the people to fly "unto Himself," to come closer to the divine sphere, up high, in heaven.

From the height of the eagle's route, the state of the nation may be seen afresh. The image of the eagles' wings is set within a poetic frame of national names. The opening parallelism begins with a call to the "house of Jacob," the most primary designation of the nation (Exod. 1 : 1), and its parallel, the "children of Israel." The move from the former to the latter captures the historical process through which Jacob's household became a people. But the most dramatic transition is evident in the leap from these designations to the three titles that appear at the end, titles that were never heard before: "peculiar treasure" (*'am segula*), "kingdom of priests" (*mamlekhet cohanim*), and "holy nation" (*goy kadosh*). These tokens of chosenness are offered to the children of Israel provided that they obey God's covenant. The people seem eager to step into this new position: they answer at once—and together (*yachdav*)—accepting the divine offer, committing themselves to the Law as they commit themselves to each other.

The initiatory dimension of the eagle metaphor is elaborated in the Song of Moses:

He found him in a desert region,
In an empty howling waste.
He engirded him, watched over him,
Guarded him as the pupil of His eye.
Like an eagle who rouses his nestlings,
Gliding down to his young,
So did He spread His wings and take him,
Bear him along on His pinions.
(Deut. 32:10–11)[2]

Much as eagles catch their young on their backs while initiating them in flying, so God bears the Israelites on His wings, "rousing" His offspring, spurring them to dare the flight, to mount toward the heights of sacred knowledge, to transcend their lowly beginnings in the land of Egypt and become a consecrated nation.[3]

One could regard the entire period of wandering as an initiatory voyage in "an empty howling waste" through which the Father introduces his chosen firstborn son into the realm of sacred knowledge.[4] Indeed, as I claimed at the outset, metaphors of national birth, suckling, and initiation intermingle throughout the Pentateuchal account of national formation. But at Sinai, the most sacred station along the road, the most secluded site in the desert—accessible, it seems, only to those who are brought there by God—the Israelites undergo rites that bear a more pronounced resemblance to initiation rites. Above all, they bear resemblance to initiation rites at the onset of puberty whose role is to mark the boy's turning away from childhood and entrance into the world of social responsibilities.[5] Such rites often involve a period of seclusion, a "liminal" phase, to use Arnold van Gennep's terms, in which the initiates are taken to an isolated zone, where the sacred codes and customs of the community are revealed to them.[6]

In exploring the initiatory aspects of Sinai, I will take into account not only the memorable scenes of revelation but also the subsequent rites that were performed on this mountain: the feast around the Golden Calf and the ceremonious construction of the Tabernacle.[7] In doing so, I rely on Victor Turner's consideration of ritual as a *process*, "open to the play of thought, feeling, and will."[8] Rituals, Turner suggests, provide areas of time and space for social reflexivity. "In them are generated new models, often fantastic, some of which may have sufficient power and plausibility to replace eventually the force-backed political and jural models that control the centers of a society's ongoing life."[9] Novices, accordingly, are not merely blank slates on which the elders inscribe consecrated cultural laws but active participants who—especially during the liminal phase—may fashion new social models while questioning the validity of the sacred corpus that is passed down to them.[10]

My reading, however, goes beyond anthropological issues. I provide an extensive *textual* analysis, considering the literary dimension of the rites: the ways in which the writers of Exodus chose to shape this historical moment.[11] Here as before, biblical historiography provides a sharp interpretation of national events, recording both the highlights and the crises at stake. Sinai represents a time of love, of great intimacy, between the Father and the son, ignited by the son's advance toward the Father's world. And yet, as we shall see, the threshold of adolescence is at the same time a very violent site, where the nation's growing powers and growing desires lead to fierce and gory clashes with the Father.

Revelation

The consent of the people to become a titled nation is followed by the most dramatic scene of all: God's descent. This is the only time in the history of Israel when such a grand revelation takes place. If so far the nation ascended toward God, or the mountain of God, now in a moment of unparalleled intimacy God descends upon the mountain: first through a cloud and flashes of lightning and then through a fire that sets the entire site ablaze. Sounds of thunder and the blare of the horn, growing louder and louder, intermingle with the wondrous sights. The people tremble with excitement and horror in response to God's overwhelming appearance—and so does the smoking mountain (the same verb *vayecherad*, "quaked" or "trembled," is used in both cases—Exod. 19:16–18).

It is an ecstatic experience in which the divine and the human worlds come close, but precisely because of this unusual proximity, certain rules must be strictly observed. Flying at the appropriate height, as Daedalus warns his son, Icarus, is an art. Those who venture to exceed human limits, or misjudge their power, can only lose their feathers in the terrible heat of heaven and fall into the deep. The people are required to follow Moses' instructions meticulously in preparation for the event: they must purify themselves, wash their clothes, refrain from sexual relations, and, above all, resist the temptation to climb the mountain. "Take heed to yourselves, that ye go not up into the mount, or touch the border of it: whosoever toucheth the mount shall be surely put to death" (19:12). The peculiar prohibition against "touching" here and in the next verse (19:13) discloses the illicit—somewhat incestuous—desire that such initiatory moments generate: to draw even nearer to the divine, to become one with God, to touch His body.[12] But just as sexual relations in the human sphere are regulated, so too the contact between the human and the divine is confined. Moses "set bounds about the mount" (19:23). A careless glance at the divine realm, let alone touch, means death. Sacred intimacy is at the same time the heart of horror and the greatest desire of all.

The erotic quality of the bond between God and Israel is the specialty of the Husband-wife metaphor, as developed by the Prophets, but it is nonetheless an essential ingredient—if less apparent—of the Pentateuchal renditions of the Father-son relationship. That the Father is something of a Mother in this case only adds, I suspect, to the erotic tension at Mount Sinai. Somewhere along the slopes of this mountain, after all, lies the rock of Horev, the maternal rock that yielded sweet refreshing water for the thirsty congregation in Exodus 17. Do the people crave, among other things, to touch the rocky breasts of the deity?[13]

Various individual rites of initiation hover in the background. Jacob engages in a daringly physical initiatory struggle with a mysterious divine man from whom he wrests a new name, the name of the nation: Israel. But the most relevant individual rite is that of Moses at the burning bush.[14] "When thou hast brought forth the people out of Egypt, ye shall serve God upon this mountain," says God to Moses through the flames, foretelling the nation's initiation as He designates the terror-stricken Moses as His special messenger (Exod. 3:12). And indeed the nation's initiation takes place on the same "holy ground" where Moses took off his shoes and marveled at the wondrous bush (*seneh*), burning with fire yet unconsumed. The pun that links "Sinai" and "seneh" highlights the connection between the two scenes.[15] The unique fire that "devours" the top of Mount Sinai (24:17) evokes the fire in the midst of the seneh. It is, however, an intensified version of the earlier sight: this time the mountain itself burns, not merely a bush. This time God reveals himself to the community as a whole and demands that the entire nation, not only Moses, become His special servant.

Communitas: The Question of Social Hierarchies

The unusual proximity between the divine and human realms at Sinai is accompanied by the blurring of social hierarchies. Each member of the community assumes the status of a priest and is deemed worthy of approaching the divine. Much as the priest is allowed to go up by the steps of the altar (provided that he covers his nakedness) to a site no one else is allowed to enter (see Exod. 20:26, 28:42–43), so the people as a whole, being a "kingdom of priests," may enter the sacred zone of the mountain of God and witness His descent. Theophany is communal: it is not only the privilege of the elite but rather a spectacle accessible to all. Turner regards such suspension of social hierarchies in initiation rites as an instance of "communitas."[16] Communitas, he suggests, designates "a moment in and out of time, in and out of secular social structure, which reveals, however fleetingly, some recognition (in symbol if not always in language) of a generalized social bond."[17]

The egalitarian bent of the Sinai revelation is underscored in Deuteronomy:

> Ye stand this day all of you before the Lord your God; your captains of your tribes, your elders, and your officers, with all the men of Israel. Your little ones, your wives, and thy stranger that is in thy camp, from the hewer of the wood unto the drawer of thy water. (29:10–13)

No one should be prevented from entering the covenant with God. Even women, children, strangers, and lowly servants who fetch wood and water are expected to take part in the ceremony.

Judith Plaskow sees Sinai as the ultimate moment of exclusion vis-à-vis women.[18] She interprets the prohibition to approach women on this occasion as an indication of the patriarchal character of the covenant. One cannot ignore the underlying patriarchal presuppositions of the biblical text, but Sinai, of all places, is a station where hierarchies are momentarily challenged in gender terms as well. The ban on sexual relations is meant primarily to restrict the contact between the human and divine realms—not to exclude women from the scene. The mountain too, after all, was not to be touched.

Social hierarchies, however, are suspended rather than abolished. Alongside the representations of communitas one finds scenes that reaffirm social differentiation as they distinguish between various levels of revelation. Different members of the community seem to have different abilities and (in)sights. While the people remain at the foot of Mount Sinai, the elders (with Moses, Aaron, Nadav, and Abihu) are allowed to go up the mountain to a point from which they can get a closer glimpse of God.[19] In the account of the elders' voyage up the slope, Buber writes, "the narrator breaks into rhythmic words, as though he were quoting verses from a time-old song."[20]

> And they saw the God of Israel: and there was under his feet as it were a paved work of a sapphire stone, and as it were the body of heaven in his clearness. And upon the nobles of the children of Israel he laid not his hand: also they saw God, and did eat and drink. (Exod. 24:10–11)

The poem offers an audacious depiction of human-divine familiarity. The nobles are granted the sight of the treasures that lie under God's feet—the sapphire stone and its poetic parallel: heavenly splendor. They "see" and "eat" and "drink" at once in a striking encounter between the spiritual and the physical.[21]

Moses is the most privileged of all. He climbs up the mountain time and again and engages in a direct dialogue with God: "And the Lord spake unto Moses face to face, as a man speaketh unto his friend" (33:11). The boundary between the divine and the human spheres in this case almost dissolves: Moses and God converse on the same plane, as two friends. The nobles had a vision of the realm below God's feet, Moses gets as far as God's face.[22]

In one of the greatest moments of intimacy between the two, God reveals His inscriptions to Moses. The first set of Tablets, "written with the finger of God" (31:18), is given to Moses in a most tangible way, as if transferred from hand to hand. The second set of Tablets, fashioned by Moses after the model of the primary one, is no less inspiring. The contact with the splendor of the divine word was so powerful this time that the skin of Moses' face "shone" as he came down the mountain with the new Tablets in his hands (34:29).

The People of the Book

Stephen Dedalus, the protagonist of James Joyce's *A Portrait of the Artist as a Young Man*, had an ecstatic revelation one day:

> His throat ached with a desire to cry aloud, the cry of a hawk or eagle on high, to cry piercingly of his deliverance to the winds. . . . An instant of wild flight had delivered him and the cry of triumph which his lips withheld cleft his brain—Stephaneforos! . . . He was alone. He was unheeded, happy and near to the wild heart of life. . . . A girl stood before him in midstream. . . . She seemed like one whom magic had changed into the likeness of a strange and beautiful seabird. . . . Her thighs, fuller and softhued as ivory, were bared almost to the hips where the white fringes of her drawers were like featherings of soft white down. . . . Her bosom was as a bird's soft and slight, slight and soft as the breast of some darkplumaged dove . . . and a faint flame trembled on her cheek. . . . Her image had passed into his soul for ever and no word had broken the holy silence of his ecstasy. Her eyes had called him and his soul had leaped at the call. To live, to err, to fall, to triumph, to recreate life out of life![23]

For Joyce, who draws both on the myth of Daedalus and on the Bible, initiation entails an erotic encounter with the divine, an invitation to leap up toward the soft and luring bosom of a semi-bare "bird"—whether the bird is internal ("the cry of an eagle") or external—like the girl by the sea. The climactic moment of Stephen's ecstasy, however, is the realization that to follow the call of the androgynous bird means to venture "to recreate life out of life," to be a writer.

The revelation at Mount Sinai culminates in the creation of

multifarious texts.[24] Indeed, the unique feature of the Sinaic initiation rites is the extent to which they revolve around writing. It is not art in the modern sense of the word, for God is the Author, and the text is divine. Nonetheless, human hands take part in the production. Moses' contribution is indisputable, but to some extent the congregation as a whole participates in the translation of divine sights into texts. Israel is more of a young priest than a young artist, but the two positions are not mutually exclusive. Being God's servant does not preclude art. Art—and writing in particular—seems to be an invaluable medium for those who wish to soar up after the Father. To write is to imitate God.

At Sinai the Israelites become the people of the Book, bound to God and to each other through a set of sacred texts.[25] In yet another ceremony conducted at the foot of the mountain, by a newly built altar of twelve pillars, Moses writes God's words in a book called *sefer habrit*, the book of the covenant, and then reads it aloud to the surrounding audience. The scene takes place right after God's descent and before the carving of the first set of Tablets. Moses

> took the book of the covenant, and read in the audience of the people: and they said, All that the Lord hath said will we do, and be obedient. And Moses took the blood, and sprinkled it on the people, and said, Behold the blood of the covenant, which the Lord hath made with you concerning all these words. (24:7–8)

The book plays a significant role in the making of the solemn covenant between God and Israel. On hearing the words of the text, the people answer in "one voice," saying *na'ase venishma* (literally, we will do and hear / obey), reversing the expected order of the verbs, underlining their desire to accept the book and do as God commands, unconditionally.[26] They commit themselves to an ongoing dialogue, to "hearing" with no temporal limitations, "until all and everlasting time."[27]

What were the contents of the book of the covenant? Exodus provides no detailed account (this is true of the two sets of Tablets as well). Most scholars assume that the book of the covenant included the laws that precede the ceremony. Some suggest that this legislative corpus was accompanied by a written testimony commemorating the terms of the covenant.[28] But law goes hand in hand with narrative in the biblical text, and for this very reason one can hardly draw the boundaries of the book.[29] The book consists of God's words and laws, we are told, which may well include the poetic depictions of revelation in Exodus 19. What is more, the very act of making a covenant calls to mind other covenantal stories: above all, the covenant between God and Abraham in Genesis 15 and its reaffirmation in the flesh through circumcision in Genesis 17. The covenant has a history that is necessarily inscribed in the book, however implicitly. The emphasis placed on law at Sinai need not be taken literally. What it seems to suggest above all is that narrative is as binding as law and that law has a history.

Moses sprinkles blood before and after the reading: on the altar with the twelve pillars—representing the twelve tribes—and on the surrounding people. Israel was marked by blood on the night of the Exodus, when the Destroyer passed over the houses of the Hebrews (Exod. 12). Birthmarks, however, require remarking at later stages as well.[30] Israel's chosenness needs to be reaffirmed now that it has reached a more advanced stage of national formation. The amorphous multitude of fleeing slaves has transformed into a structured confederacy of twelve tribes with an intricate and extensive apparatus of laws and narratives.

Birth and rebirth are familiar initiatory themes. Death symbolizes a violent break with the past and underlines the intensity of transformation that the initiates undergo as they move from one stage to the next. In certain Australian tribes the novices are considered dead for the first part of the ceremony (which lasts a fairly long time) and are then resurrected and taught how to live, but differently than in childhood.[31] In the Wiradjuri initiation ceremonies the boys are symbolically "killed" or "swallowed" by a Divine Being or a monster who then resuscitates them with one tooth missing.[32] The Israelites come close to death on witnessing God's shocking descent, but their exposure to the divine, with its horror and beauty, ultimately leads to a scene of national rebirth in which the entire community enters a new textual world.

The Golden Calf: The Laughter of the People

Rites of initiation are constructed and deconstructed at a dazzling pace at this station. When Moses goes up the mountain for forty days and forty nights the people who remain below break the law without hesitation. Moses is far too detached from his community, they seem to claim, and so is his God. They seek a different kind of leader and a different set of religious practices. "The people gathered themselves together unto Aaron, and said unto him, Up, make us gods, which shall go before us; for as for this Moses, the man that brought us up out of the land of Egypt, we wot not what is become of him" (Exod. 32 : 1). Aaron yields to popular demand, collects earrings from all the members of the community (women and children included), and fashions a golden calf. The people welcome the Calf with a cry of joy: "This is your god, O Israel, who brought you up out of the land of Egypt!" (32:4).[33] In the ceremonial lines with which God first addresses the nation, He presents Himself as the one who brought Israel out of Egypt. It takes but forty days for the people to twist God's words: first in defining Moses as the one who delivered them and then—far worse—in regarding a golden calf as the emblem of their Savior.[34]

God is incensed. Disappointed by Israel's swift "turning aside," He reconsiders His bond with the people. "I have seen this people," He says to Moses, "and behold, it is a stiffnecked people: Now therefore let me alone, that my wrath may wax hot against them, and that I may consume them: and I will make of thee a great nation" (32:9–10). The fire that devoured the top of the mountain a few days earlier as a token of God's passionate love now turns into a deadly, all-consuming, fire of wrath. If it were not for Moses' plea, God would have destroyed the people on the spot, shaping another nation in their stead through Moses. Isaiah's verse "I reared children and brought them up / And they have rebelled against me!" (1:2) may highlight God's feelings at this point.[35] The son He had just endowed with the highest titles of all—"holy nation," "peculiar treasure," "kingdom of priests"—is nothing but a reckless rebel who is incapable of grasping the great value of divine knowledge or of appreciating God's efforts on his behalf.[36] The only national title God deems truly suitable for the sinful nation is "stiffnecked"—and this is, one should bear in mind, the moment in which the nation's stiff neck is invented. Israel's growing body resists the Father's will more than ever before.

Joshua, who hears the voices of the joyful people from afar, misinterprets them. "There is a cry of war in the camp," he says with great concern to Moses. Moses responds gravely: "It is not the sound of the tune [*'anot*] of triumph, or the sound of the tune [*'anot*] of defeat; it is the sound of song [*'anot*] that I hear" (32:17–18).[37] The singing of the people, Moses claims, is not yoked to the different genres of war songs, or to any other genre whatsoever. This is the sound of singing, *'anot,* that is so wild, formless, and agonizing that one can hardly define it. Moses' response is abrupt. The pain seems to be so great that he cannot find the words to convey his enormous frustration. The people have betrayed him. They have failed to learn. How can one build a nation with a crowd that lacks even the most elementary sense of discipline?

On reaching the camp, Moses sees what God had seen earlier: a feast the focus of which is a golden calf. The anger that cut Moses' voice on hearing the people flares up on seeing them. He casts the Tablets out of his hands, breaking them "beneath the mount," where the covenant was made (32:19). The breaking of the Tablets of the covenant is a sharp response that mirrors the people's breaking of the law. Later Moses (who oscillates between rage and compassion) will ask God to blot him out of His book (the Torah? the Book of Life?—32:33) in the course of yet another plea on behalf of the people. God makes clear that He will erase from the book only the names of those who have sinned. At Sinai the Israelites become the people of the Book, but there is an ongoing threat that this text may be demolished, or else that the nation's name will be blotted out of God's Book. Reaching the holy mountain does not guarantee the nation's holiness. Topographic heights may coincide with spiritual heights, but not necessarily. The Bible clearly refrains from turning this locus into a fetish. The people "fall" despite the fact that they have remained at the very same site.

But are the people truly interested in breaking the covenant? What they seem to demand, above all, is a redefinition of its terms. At this rare moment the people do not ask to return to Egypt but rather to borrow some of Egypt's cultural heritage as they construct their own. Instead of wiping out their cultural past, they wish to refashion it in a way that would acknowledge both their departure from and debt to Egyptian culture. They long for Egypt's rich and sophisticated world of representations as much as they yearn for its fleshpots. The commandment that forbids them to make a "graven image, or any likeness of any thing that is in heaven above, or that is in the earth beneath, or that is in the water under the earth"(20:4) is too restrictive as far as they are concerned. They want images, not only words. The Calf is a syncretic hybrid artifact. While displaying certain pagan features, it equally bears the stamp of national history in commemorating Israel's Exodus from Egypt (32:4). Against the Mosaic privileging of the Word, the people set up an image, fashioning the covenant by visual means as well, adding another medium to the cultural contours of the nation.[38]

The change in representational modes is accompanied by a change in the style of feasting. The flamboyant celebration around the Calf stands in sharp contrast to the solemn rites that precede it. The people eat the meat of the sacrifices, drink, sing, dance, and rise "to play" (32:6). The verb *vayetsachek*, which the King James Version translates as "play," may also mean "laugh," "joke," "mock," "ridicule," and "flirt."[39] If we follow the people's perspective—rather than the official one—the great merriment at the foot of Mount Sinai is a vital protest against the unbearable seriousness of the official initiatory ceremonies. In the most solemn moment in the biography of ancient Israel, the laughter of the people bursts out, calling for a more sensuous carnivalesque mode of communal celebration. With its broad range of meanings, *vayetsachek* calls to mind Mikhail Bakhtin's notion of carnival laughter. "Carnival laughter," Bakhtin writes, "is the laughter of all the people. . . . The entire world is seen in its droll aspect. . . . [I]t is gay, triumphant, and at the same time mocking, deriding. It asserts and denies, it buries and revives."[40] Such laughter, he goes on to suggest, expresses the people's deep distrust of official truth, their criticism of the rigid austerity that characterizes religious festivities. Its role, however, is not merely to negate but also to revive: to add vigor to communal life and give rise to cultural change and regeneration.

Earlier I regarded the choice of a calf for an idol as an expression of longings vis-à-vis an absent Mother. I would now like to add another layer of interpretation to this image. Perhaps the fact that the people choose to worship a calf—rather than a bull—stems from their desire to replace the stern and ever-demanding Father (be it God or Moses), who is either overbearing or absent, and put on the pedestal, in His stead, the lively dreams of the Son.[41] The nestling on the eagle's pinions—to return for a moment to the metaphor with which we began—insists on his right to laugh, to say more than "I do and obey," to sing freely as he takes off, to take part in determining the national route of flight.

The Mountain and the Cask

Initiation, apparently, is not merely a smooth flight toward the divine. Sinai, among other things, is a site of intense ambivalence.

The Golden Calf episode underscores the ambivalence that is already noticeable in the people's demand in Exodus 20:16 that Moses serve as a buffer between them and heaven: "You speak to us," they say to Moses, "and we will obey; but let not God speak to us, lest we die." God's loud, imposing voice is more than their ears can endure, and His relentless listing of laws leaves them breathless.

Several midrashim touch on the coercive dimension of Sinai. One midrash describes the people leaving the mountain as a "child running away from school."[42] A similar midrash suggests that "when the Israelites were finally allowed to leave the holy mountain they rose early, folded their tents, packed their belongings, and marched as fast as they could—not for one day, as they were commanded, but for three days. They didn't want any more laws."[43] The most renowned interpretation in this connection is a talmudic one: "And they stood under the mount. R. Abdimi b. Hama b. Hasa said: This teaches that the Holy one, blessed be He, overturned the mountain upon them like an [inverted] cask, and said to them, 'If ye accept the Torah, 'tis well; if not, there shall be your burial'" (Shabath II, 88a).

When the people commit themselves to God, they do so of their own free will with much passion: they want to be raised to a new position by the Father's side. And yet the sacred texts are delivered from above, like a heavy, menacing cask, crushing them beneath, making them wonder whether they had much of a choice to begin with. The nation that was born despite itself is also initiated despite itself. The children of Israel are "freely bound" to God, Walzer writes, but at times they feel more bound than free, which is why they try to loosen the law.[44] Alongside the desire to become one with God there is an opposite desire, equally acute, to flee the insufferable weight of the mountain and avoid such fierce intimacy. Divine love is as strong as death.

But no one who is asked to be a divine agent can escape God. It is a tyrannical offer one cannot refuse. Moses, who tries to convince God in the initiatory scene by the burning bush that he is not meant for the mission, is one such case. Jeremiah, who claims that he is but a na'ar (child or youth) and cannot deliver the Word, is another relevant example, not to mention Jonah, who runs off to the vast sea in an unsuccessful attempt to hide from God.

Bloodshed

The story of the Golden Calf ends with dreadful violence. Moses grinds the Calf to powder, turning the image of the Son's pride into dust. Then he scatters the powder upon water and makes the entire congregation drink the potion. Through this punitive ritual, he attempts to restore the superiority of the Father religion and make clear that the people must swallow their idolatrous cravings and repent.[45]

This is but the first mode of punishment. What follows is far more violent.

> Then Moses stood in the gate of the camp, and said, Who is on the Lord's side? let him come unto me. And all the sons of Levi gathered themselves together unto him. And he said unto them, . . . Put every man his sword by his side, and go in and out from gate to gate throughout the camp, and slay every man his brother, and every man his companion, and every man his neighbour. (32:26–27)

The unified nation that responded in "one voice" to God's offer is torn into pieces, so much so that even friends and brothers kill each other. The sons of Levi (the tribe of the official priests) stand by Moses (who is a member of this tribe) and assume control over the gates of the camp. Three thousand people are assassinated. The "kingdom of priests" falls apart. A select group of divine servants—the Levites are consecrated and blessed by Moses for this deed—now rules the camp, zealously slaying dissidents with their swords. And as if this were not enough, God strikes the camp with a deadly plague. The blood that was sprinkled by Moses on the people earlier was not only a mark of rebirth but also a reminder (much as the cut carcasses in Genesis 15) of the fate that awaits those who venture to violate the covenant.

Theodor Reik (who relies on Freud's observations in *Totem and Taboo*) regards puberty rites as ceremonies in which fathers and sons both express and expiate their aggressive impulses toward each other. The cruelties and mutilations that often accompany such ceremonies (circumcision being a common one), Reik argues, are meant, above all, as a threat to the growing sons who have reached the point of sexual maturity. The fathers "signify to their sons . . . that they are ready to receive them into the company of men, but only on one condition, namely, that the youths renounce their incestuous and hostile impulses."[46]

The Israelites are subject to a cruel lesson by Moses and the Levites through which they are expected to learn how to master their souls and bodies. No more flirting with calves and cows. Their illicit desires to replace the Father must be renounced if they wish to be counted among the living and maintain their chosen position. And God, in His turn (as Moses reminds Him), needs to renounce His violent urge to demolish the nation. He must show mercy and forgive. Bloodshed is to be stopped.

The Construction of the Tabernacle

The ceremonious construction of the Tabernacle, the final ritual at Sinai, adds a reconciliatory element to the story of the nation's initiation. The Father and the son renew and redefine their covenant through the fashioning of this tentlike wilderness sanctuary, with its colorful curtains, refined furniture, priestly items, and the ark at the center. God provides the people with what they asked for in the Golden Calf episode—license to make a tangible emblem of Divine Presence—and the grateful community follows the divine blueprint for the Tabernacle with unparalleled devotion. From now on God will "dwell" not only in heaven but also in the midst of the camp (the term for Tabernacle, *mishkan*, means "dwelling"). From now on the people will be defined not only by the Book but also by the spectacular sanctuary that envelops the text. The Sinaitic initiation is a slow and tumultuous process that involves writing and rewriting, breaking one set of Tablets and carving out new ones, fashioning a calf, and then building a tabernacle in its stead.

The making of the Tabernacle, I believe, is a curious cross between the official sequence of initiatory ceremonies and the popular rituals of the Golden Calf: between the solemn, lawful, character of the former and the daring materiality of the latter, between the spellbound witnessing of the revelation and the more active participation in the fashioning of the graven image, between the official privileging of writing and the popular quest for other representational modes. Critics such as Nahum Sarna who regard the Tabernacle as the very antithesis of the Calf miss the intricate cultural negotiations at stake. I do not mean to suggest that these negotiations are presented openly. In fact, the text seems to deny the extent to which the Tabernacle is indebted to the Calf. Thus the strange split between the lengthy depiction of the building instructions (Exod. 25–31) and the lengthy depiction of the construction itself (Exod. 35–40) may be seen as an attempt to undermine the impact of the people's demands and to suggest that God, from the outset, even before the Golden Calf episode, intended to provide a tangible emblem of Divine Presence.

The most conspicuous representatives of the Calf in the Tabernacle are the cherubim, the golden, winged creatures (semibird, semihuman) set above the ark cover, whose image is lavishly duplicated on the colorful cloths of the Tabernacle as well as on the *parokhet*, the embroidered partitioning curtain.[47] The outline of the graven images adorning the ark is provided in detail:

> And thou shalt make two cherubim of gold, of beaten work shalt thou make them, in the two ends of the mercy seat [the cover of the ark]. And make one cherub on the one end, and the other cherub on the other end: even of the mercy seat shall ye make cherubims on the two ends thereof. And the cherubims shall stretch forth their wings on high, covering the mercy seat with their wings, and their faces shall look one to another; toward the mercy seat shall the faces of the cherubims be. (25:18–20)

Much like the Golden Calf, the cherubim pose a clear violation of the prohibition against images. They are made of gold (here too the people's collected jewelry is the source of gold), of "beaten work," and represent visually that which is in heaven above (birds) and on the earth beneath (human beings). The Law, in other words, is more pliable than it may first seem. To mitigate the provocative quality of the cherubim by claiming that these creatures do not impinge on the prohibitions of the Decalogue—given that they are the product of the imagination (rather than imitations of real beings), or that they are merely a symbolic representation of God's throne (something that may have been true of the Calf as well)—is to overlook a central point, however paradoxical: God is capable of breaking the Law.[48] At this point, He does so in response to the people's quest for images.

But then God violates the letter of the Law, not its spirit. The construction of the cherubim is ordained by God to serve Him and, as such, is by definition consecrated.[49] And given that the cherubim are created in keeping with divine will, every detail is momentous, every angle needs to be rendered with utmost precision. "Aaron makes the Calf so quickly that the object is there in less than a sentence."[50] By contrast, the design of the cherubim, like their actual making (37:7–9), is displayed in a slow, ceremonious pace with rhythmic repetitions.

On second look the cherubim are not only a peculiar parallel of the Calf but also a continuation of the opening initiatory scenes. The wings of the cherubim "stretching forth on high," ready to take off toward heaven, call to mind the eagle metaphor. Indeed, the dialogue that began in Exodus 19 is to be continued in the vacant space between the cherubim, above the ark, where God will "meet" (*veno'adeti*) the people through His voice. The cherubim are not set apart on a pedestal but rather serve as the guardians of the Word, be it the voice from above or the Tablets below. Their long protective wings shield (*sokhekhim*) the divine texts, underlining their sacredness. Writing in the Tabernacle blends with, and is enhanced by, the sights that surround it.

One of the most intriguing mixtures of words and images in the Tabernacle is to be found on the *efod*, the garment of the high priest, and the *choshen*, the breastplate of judgment that is attached to it. The ephod and the breastplate (like the curtains of the Tabernacle) are made of colorful cloths: blue, purple, scarlet, and "fine twined linen." But the most marvelous feature in each one of these priestly items is a set of twelve precious stones, bearing the names of the twelve tribes of Israel. The following passage depicts the stones on the breastplate, but a similar set is placed on the "shoulders" of the ephod.

> And thou shalt set in it settings of stones, even four rows of stones: the first row shall be a sardius, a topaz, and a carbuncle: this shall be the first row. And the second row shall be an emerald, a sapphire, and a diamond. . . . And the stones shall be with the names of the children of Israel, twelve, according to their names, like the engravings of a signet. . . . And Aaron shall bear the names of the children of Israel in the breastplate of judgment upon his heart, when he goeth in unto the holy place, for a memorial before the Lord continually. (28:17–29)

The engraved names capture the splendor of the titles bestowed on Israel in the opening scene. They display the chosenness of the nation: as if Israel, God's "peculiar treasure," were as glamorous as precious stones, as admirable as the sublime sapphirelike beauties under God's feet (see Exod. 24:10). These artful signets, which serve as a memorial of the covenant, take part in the intimate exchange of the high priest with God. The priest, who covers his loins with the ephod and wears the twelve stones on his heart, represents the nation as a whole on entering the holy of holies.

What the breastplate and the ephod prove is that words and images need not be set apart: they can shed light on each other. The people who "saw the sounds" (*ro'im 'et ha-kolot;* Exod. 20:15) in the moment of theophany may now "see the letters," or at least the exquisite artifacts surrounding the inscriptions. The Zohar highlights the exhilarating visualization of writing at Sinai. The letters on the Tablets, according to the Zohar, are the greatest sight of all: full of light, color, and movement.

> The moment these letters came forth,
> secretly circling as one,
> a spark flashed out to engrave. . . .
> Sparks burst into flashes, up high and down below,
> then quieted down and rose up high, beyond, beyond.
> The flow measured out ten cubits on the other side,
> and comets shot out in colors like before.
> And so on every side. . . .
> All of Israel saw the letters
> flying through space in every direction,
> engraving themselves on the tablets of stone.[51]

The Zohar marvels at the visual power of the Tablets, but the colors and cubits (the measuring unit of the Tabernacle's plan) in this reading seem to evoke the sanctuary as well, pointing to the affinity between the two works.

Cultural Poetics[52]

The construction of the Tabernacle is an ars poetic moment in the text that reveals much about the biblical perception of art as it comments on the intricacies of initiation. The sacred knowledge of the community is not a fixed corpus, the invention of a select circle, but rather the product of extensive negotiations between different socioideological groups, different beliefs, and different dreams. It is the product of collective imagination and collective work. The community as a whole, here more clearly than in the preceding rites, is something of a young artist, groping for the right mode of expression.

When God first provides Moses with the blueprint for the Tabernacle, he suggests that Bezalel and his assistant, Aholiab, be in charge of the work. He promises to "fill" Bezalel "with the spirit of God, in wisdom, and in understanding, and in knowledge, and in all manner of workmanship" (31:3). But such divine inspiration is not merely an individual gift. God also "puts wisdom" "in the hearts of all that are wisehearted" (*chakam lev*). Many are the wise hearted in the community. Even the anonymous women who participate in the work are defined as "wise hearted." Being an artist requires a special kind of wisdom that emanates from the heart, regardless of class or gender. The heart features in another expression that is used in this connection. The artistic offerings for the Tabernacle must be given wholeheartedly, "And they came, both men and women, as many as were willing hearted" (35:22; see also 25:2, 35:21). Art is not only a matter of competence or means, it must involve a willing gesture to contact the divine, that is, internal readiness to receive divine wisdom. Only those whose heart is open may take part in the sacred building of God's sanctuary, the heart of the community.

The communal character of the work is laid out with loving detail. Everyone is invited to contribute in his or her own way. Those who had wood brought acacia wood. Others brought bracelets, earrings, and rings. The wealthier princes (*nesi'im*) "brought onyx stones, and stones to be set, for the ephod, and for the breastplate" (35:27). Women who were "wise hearted did spin with their hands, and brought that which they had spun, both of blue, and of purple, and of scarlet, and of fine linen" (35:25). Other women, who assembled (*tsov'ot*) by the opening of the tent (cultic attendants?), donated their brass mirrors for the making of the priestly basin (38:8).[53] Instead of beautifying their bodies, garments, or tents, the people devoted their gems and skills, with much enthusiasm, to creating an image of their communion.

The making of the sanctuary seems to mirror the making of the biblical text. The Bible, as biblical scholarship has taught us, is most likely a patchwork of diverse sources brought together. It is, as Alter shows in his remarkable discussion of the art of biblical narrative, an artistic patchwork, a case of "composite artistry" that required sensitive editing of the different traditions.[54] The Tabernacle makes visible the ways in which composite and collective artistry may be carried out: a leading team and numerous contributors from all walks of life. One need not limit the contributors of the biblical text to J, E, P, and D, as the advocates of the "documentary hypothesis" suggest, or to written traditions alone. Oral traditions probably found their way into the Book, though in modified form. Even if the Book—far more than the

Tabernacle—bears the stamp of the official religion, it nonetheless gives expression to a whole gamut of perspectives.

It would be misleading to imply that the fashioning of the sacred corpus of ancient Israel always relied on tranquil collective work and blissful moments of communitas. The debate over the appropriate mode of representation that led to the invention of the Tabernacle was undoubtedly a fierce one. And one may assume that the making of the Book, likewise, involved instances of tense conflict. While the explicit poetics of the biblical text puts forth a willing heart as a prerequisite for art, the implicit poetics seems to point to the stiff neck as another indispensable source of inspiration.

New representations, both verbal and nonverbal, are generated in the course of the Sinaitic initiatory rites; some gain sufficient power to become canonized, others are rejected or modified, some are transferred from one medium to another while others remain within a demarcated zone, a few are wild departures while the bulk are more restrained, some intermingle harmoniously while others clash with vigor—all take part in defining the cultural character of the young nation.

The Return of the Mother

In *Moses and Monotheism,* Freud provides a comparison between the spiritual growth of a child and the development of monotheism.

> The progress in spirituality consists in deciding against the direct sense perception in favor of the so-called higher intellectual processes—that is to say, in favor of memories, reflection and deduction. An example of this would be the

> decision that paternity is more important than maternity, although the former cannot be proved by the senses as the latter can. This is why the child has to have the father's name and inherit after him. Another example would be: our God is the greatest and mightiest, although he is invisible like the storm and the soul.[55]

Just as a child (or rather a boy) must leave his mother behind and inherit after the father, so ancient Israel, Freud argues, eventually rejected the world of the senses and endorsed the spiritually advanced world of the invisible abstract Father.[56] Freud's observations raise a number of problems. To begin with, the biblical text does not attribute to God absolute transcendence. The stricture on making images of God does not mean that God is invisible. Rather it insists that the *reproduction* of His image visually is forbidden.[57] Sinai serves as decisive proof—from the scene of revelation to the construction of the Tabernacle—that the senses were part and parcel of religious life in ancient Israel. God is not only associated with the storm and the word but also with the visual and the concrete.

Let us focus, however, on Freud's notion of national development as a transition from the realm of the mother to that of the father. *Moses and Monotheism* opens with thought-provoking displacements of identity (Moses is construed as an Egyptian), but at this point of the argument, Freud seems to succumb to the temptation of linear plots.[58] His account of spiritual progress may shed light on the official ideal of national development, but this is only one thread in the nation's patchwork. Other social forces apparently strove for a different definition of the sublime that allotted more room for the maternal in heaven. The Father, after all, embodies maternal facets (however limited they may be), making it rather difficult to map out a coherent line of progress in gender terms. In the discussion on national suckling, I suggested that weaning is terminable and interminable, that the Father's insistence on tearing off the "child" from the Egyptian fleshpots does not preclude His attempt to produce maternal alternatives: sweet honey in the rocks, heavenly manna, and ultimately a land of milk and honey.

Similarly, the Sinaitic initiation is not merely a story about a clear-cut separation from the maternal (though initiatory ceremonies occasionally mark precisely such a break).[59] The realm of sacred knowledge is primarily a paternal realm but not entirely so. Maternal elements may be detected on the rock of Horev, on the Golden Calf, and perhaps, most conspicuously, in the Tabernacle. The Tabernacle, among other things, pays tribute, if hidden, to the feminine aspects of the deity. The significant role women have in the ritualistic construction of the sanctuary reinforces this notion. But there is more. Perhaps the sense of plentitude, even surplus, with which the Tabernacle is built intimates that one no longer needs to strike rocks to find maternal treasures. The Mother is somehow present in the Tent, found again, which is why reparation is possible, which is why everything flows with abundance. Eager to contribute to the making of the sanctuary, the people bring more than enough, so much so that Moses proclaims throughout the camp, "Let neither man nor woman make any more work for the offering of the sanctuary. . . . For the stuff they had was sufficient for all the work to make it, and too much" (36:6–7). The Tabernacle is a luminous treasure Tent that outdoes, for a moment at least, the shadow of scarcity, the acute thirst and hunger, that haunts the Israelites throughout the wanderings in the wilderness. Wounds of weaning turn into artifacts with precious scarlet stones. Death is warded off by the flutter of the cherubim's wings on the copious colorful cloths that make the Tent.[60]

The Winged Isis

All this leads me back to Isis—not only to Isis, the suckling goddess, but also to Isis in her role as Winged Savior. Isis gained renown as a savior for her magnificent rescuing of her husband-brother, Osiris. Osiris, initially the divine ruler of Egypt, was murdered and then cut to pieces by his jealous brother, Seth. Isis wandered about devotedly and gathered the severed body parts. She then brought Osiris back to life again by waving her wings and uttering magical formulas. Osiris's resurrection is often depicted in Egyptian art. Isis appears either in human form with long wings behind the bier of the deceased or as a hawk (at times a kite) above Osiris's body. Isis's wings also provide Horus with protection, as is evident in paintings in which the latter is seated on his throne, shielded by his mother.[61]

Would it be too wild a flight of the imagination to suggest that Isis's grand, colorful wings loom large behind the mountain of God like a primary memory of a grand protective Mother in dim twilight? Egyptian religion is not more matriarchal per se (as Freud implies). But perhaps it is remembered as such. There was once an era in which the Mother was greater than life. When the memory of Egypt's guardian goddesses seeps into the biblical text, it does so with the unusual power of a repressed cultural past coming back. Monotheistic censorship may have wrenched apart Isis's wings, but it could not do away with the traces. Isis's plumage seems to turn up in modified form behind the wings of the eagle in Exodus 19, behind the wings of the cherubim in the Tabernacle —and, even more mysteriously, behind the wings of Zipporah.

Zipporah

If Yocheved is the one who most clearly resembles Isis in her role as the suckling goddess, Zipporah, Moses' wife, calls to mind the Winged Savior. Zipporah, one should bear in mind, means "bird" in Hebrew, and this is but one feature that points to her affinity with the goddess. Much like Isis, Zipporah plays the role of a savior, rescuing her husband from the wrath of a persecuting deity. The scene of rescue takes place in a strange dramatic night, right after Moses' initiation by the burning bush. God, who had just sent Moses back to Egypt to do wonders before Pharaoh and the people, suddenly attacks his messenger at a lodging along the road. Zipporah springs out of the dark and intervenes with unexpected force. She moves swiftly, takes a flint in her hand, circumcises her son, and touches "his feet" (Moses' feet? her son's?) with the foreskin, saying repeatedly: "You are truly a bridegroom of blood to me!" (*chatan damim 'ata li;* Exod. 4:25).[62] Yahweh succumbs to Zipporah's magical act and withdraws. Moses is saved.[63]

The story of "The Bridegroom of Blood" offers a perplexing counterpart to the episode by the burning bush. Here too, as in the nation's biography, initiation is a process that requires more than one rite and more than one representation. Moses' initial refusal to assume the position of deliverer in Exodus 3 turns into an eerie combat in Exodus 4, for here God's anger is conveyed by means of concrete violence and His insistence on having total possession of the one He had chosen comes close to murder.

Zipporah's intervention, however, is the most radical supplement. It seems to suggest that a feminine touch must be added before Moses' initiation can be regarded as complete. Zipporah designates Moses ceremoniously as her "bridegroom of blood" and takes him, as it were, under her wings. Women (and mothers in particular)—despite, or rather because of, their powerlessness—often have an important role in teaching weak and threatened young heroes how to handle hostile paternal figures. Rebekah offers such help to young Jacob in his struggle to assume the position of the chosen firstborn against Isaac's will.

That Zipporah's opponent is the Father Himself makes her move all the more startling. She placates Yahweh by complying partially and cunningly with His whims. Her strategy is synecdochic: *pars pro toto,* a foreskin and a touch of blood for the victim's life.[64] If she can ward off divine violence, she seems to assert, so can Moses. The mission will take its bloody toll. There will be times in which he'll feel as helpless as his son that night (is this why the two almost merge here?), as helpless as he felt back then in the ark. The transition to the position of the national leader will be slow and frustrating. But he can bloody do it! Pharaoh, like Yahweh, will ultimately let go. She marks Moses (or her son) with blood, foreshadowing the two scenes in which the nation is marked by blood: on the night of the Exodus and then again on accepting the book of the covenant at Sinai. The history of the people is already inscribed on his body and the body of their son. He must go on.

Zipporah is sent off by Moses after this nocturnal episode, and we do not hear of her until she returns to the camp in Exodus 18: "Then Jethro, Moses' father in law, took Zipporah, Moses' wife, after he [Moses] had sent her back" and came with her and her sons "unto Moses into the wilderness, where he encamped at the mount of God" (2–5). Why Zipporah was sent back remains a mystery, but her return is even more enigmatic. One can only conjecture that her wings are necessary on this historical occasion in which the nation as a whole is about to undergo an initiation rite as fearful and violent, at points, as the rite of passage in Exodus 4. Perhaps Jethro, who provides Moses with valuable advice during his visit regarding the distribution of judicial authority, also intimates that neither Moses nor God can do without feminine presence in their respective tents.

The rabbis, in any event, sensed the quest for maternal wings—on this mountain and beyond it—and fashioned a female symbol of Divine Presence, called Shekhina. The Shekhina has wings (*kanfey ha-shekhina*) with which she shields the children of Israel wherever they may be. What is more, she is regarded as a direct continuation of the sanctuary. Indeed, both terms are derivations of the root *sh.kh.n* (dwell). Thus the verse in Exodus 25:8 "And let them make me a sanctuary; that I may dwell among them" (*ve-shakhanti be-tokham*) is seen in rabbinic interpretations as a reference to the ongoing presence of the Shekhina within the Israelite camp.[65]

A Portable Station

God's dwelling is reared up on the first day of the first month in the second year of the wanderings (Exod. 40:17), that is, on the birthday of the nation, a year after the Exodus. Its inauguration rite involves the anointment and consecration of the priests as well as the anointment and consecration of the different items in the sanctuary. Israel's long initiatory process at Sinai has come to an end. The nation is finally ready to leave the mountain. From this point on, the emblem of God's presence will travel with the children of Israel in their midst and determine the rhythm of the journey by cloud and fire:

> And when the cloud was taken up from above the tabernacle, the children of Israel went onward in all their journeys: But if the cloud were not taken up, then they journeyed not till the day that it was taken up. For the cloud of the Lord was upon the tabernacle by day, and fire was on it by night, in the sight of all the house of Israel, throughout all their journeys. (40:36)

The Tabernacle is a "portable Sinai," Gabriel Josipovici writes. "Each time the people move on they dismantle it and carry it with them; each time they stop they set it up again."[66] It allows the Israelites to take with them the revelations of Sinai beyond God's mountain on wings of cherubim. The muse is to be pursued at other stations along the road through the ups and downs of the more monotonous and dry moments of desert life.

Sinai gives rise to a wandering shrine with a portable ark rather than a fixed temple. Does this mean that it calls into question the need for an identifying soil? Can a nation thrive without a land of its own? The conflict over the Promised Land will be the topic of the next chapter. The harmonious sense of unity with which the stay at Mount Sinai ends does not hold for long.

CHAPTER FIVE

The Spies in the Land of the Giants

Restless Youth

On the threshold of Canaan, in the wilderness of Paran, Moses sends twelve representatives, one from each tribe, to explore the Promised Land. "See the land," Moses instructs them, "what it is; . . . whether it be good or bad, . . . whether it be fat or lean, whether there be wood therein, or not" (Num. 13:18–20). After forty days, the men—better known as the twelve spies—return with pomegranates, figs, and an enormous cluster of grapes held by two men. Presenting the fruits to the people, they unanimously hail the fertility of the land. "We came unto the land whither thou sentest us," they say to Moses, "and surely it floweth with milk and honey; and this is the fruit of it" (Num. 13:27). The Mosaic image of the Promised Land as a land of milk and honey seems to be confirmed. But then a fissure opens up as ten of the spies swerve from the official line and depict a land that has little to do with what had been promised. Canaan is more perplexing than anticipated: it is both good and bad, "fat" yet inhospitable. Despite the milk and the honey, they claim, it is a "land that eateth up the inhabitants thereof; and all the people that we saw in it are men of a great stature. And there we saw the giants, the sons of Anak, which come of the giants: and we were in our own sight as grasshoppers, and so we were in their sight" (Num. 13:32–33). The home of the fathers, of Abraham, Isaac, and Jacob, turned out to be a strange land, a land of menacing giants, a land of others.

Of the twelve men, only two, Joshua and Caleb, are in favor of attempting the conquest of the land. The others advise against it, saying that the Israelites are incapable of overcoming the formidable Canaanites with their huge fortified cities. The people find the "evil report" of the ten spies more convincing. They cry and protest, ready to stone their leaders once again. The promise that lured them out of Egypt now seems a sham. "Let us make a captain, and let us return into Egypt," they say to one another and turn their backs on Canaan (Num 14:4). God's wrath is kindled. The ten spies die in a plague, and the desert generation as a whole is punished for its rebellious conduct. They do not deserve to enter the land, God declares, condemning them to wander in the wilderness for forty years after the number of the days in which the spies searched the land, until their carcasses fall down.

The map of the wanderings is drastically changed. Forty years of desert life are added, which means many more stations along the road. Here, as in Sinai, there is a vertical dimension as well, with unmistakable symbolic implications. The Promised Land is set up high, the very opposite of Egypt. Egypt is a land one always "descends" to: Abraham and Sarah went down to Egypt (Gen. 12:10) when famine struck Canaan; Jacob and his sons, in their turn, did the same, settling down in Goshen with the help of

Joseph. On hearing that Joseph had been devoured by a wild beast, Jacob, whose grief is immense, wishes to go down to Sheol, to the realm of the dead, with his beloved son (Gen. 37:35) but ends up instead following him down to Egypt, the land of "the monumental cult of the dead."[1] Egypt is not an underworld strictly speaking, but it comes close to being one on turning into a house of bondage at the bottom of the world. The Exodus, for this very reason, entails a magnificent ascent: out of Egypt and up to Sinai, the mountain of God, and then to the Promised Land, home of the living and the free. Canaan is predominantly a mountainous land, much closer to God than is Egypt. The question the spies quarrel over is whether "to go up" to the Promised Land. While Joshua and Caleb insist that such a move is within their powers—"Let us go up [*'alo na'ale*] at once and possess it" (Num. 13:30)—the others refuse to climb up impossible mountains in quest of a home that is possessed by others. Such heights seem to them more deadly than Egypt's lows.

Homecoming

The spies' story is a strange tale of no return, no homecoming. The hero's final trial—the final mark of his maturation—is to return home (older and wiser) after many years of wars and wanderings (which include, at times, a voyage to the underworld) and establish himself as a glorious leader, worthy of assuming the father's position. The *Odyssey* reminds us how difficult such a homecoming may be. Agamemnon, who triumphed in the war against Troy, is murdered by his wife, Clytemnestra, on entering his palace, and Odysseus undergoes many hardships before and after he lands on the shores of Ithaca. The suitors, who have invaded

Odysseus's home, are only part of the problem. To return home means to open up questions of identity. Time has passed, and home no longer seems the same, nor does the hero who returns. The story of the return of Martin Guerre relies on its ancient precursors.[2] When Odysseus finally wakes up on the shores of Ithaca after a long period of absence, he mistakes his homeland for a foreign land:

> On his island, his father's shore, that kingly man, Odysseus,
> awoke, but could not tell what land it was . . .
> "What am I in for now?
> Whose country have I come to this time? Rough
> savages and outlaws, are they, or
> godfearing people, friendly to castaways?
> Where shall I take these things? Where take myself,
> with no guide, no directions?"
>
> (Bk. 13, 185–194)[3]

Eventually Odysseus manages to rediscover his home as he refashions his identity, but the process is a long one and requires much imagination, audacity, and caution.

Biblical heroes are expected to return as well. Abraham and Sarah come back to Canaan after their sojourn in Egypt. The story of Jacob's homecoming to Canaan, however, is the most elaborate one. After twenty years of exile spent in Aram at the household of Laban, he sets out to return to his homeland at God's command. Jacob has a big family and considerable property by now—two wives, eleven sons, many servants, and many cattle—he is no longer the helpless youth who ran away after stealing his elder brother's blessing, but nonetheless fear envelops him on the bank of the Jabbok, just before crossing the border of

Canaan. "And Jacob said, O God of my father Abraham, and God of my father Isaac, the Lord which saidst unto me, Return unto thy country, and to thy kindred, and I will deal with thee. . . . Deliver me, I pray thee, from the hand of my brother, from the hand of Esau: for I fear him, lest he will come and smite me, and the mother with the children" (Gen. 32:9–11). The blessing may be his, but the patrimony, that is, the power to hold it, is in the hands of Esau—or so it seems to Jacob on the eve of his return. The underlying fear is that the return will entail a regression to earlier times, when Jacob was indeed weaker than Esau, incapable of defending himself against the wrath of his elder sibling. Jacob, much like Odysseus, must refashion his identity in order to return home safely. A mysterious "man" helps him do so. Wrestling in the night with the divine being, he acquires a new name that marks a break with the "heel," the trickster, that he was in the past and designates his new powers. "Thy name shall be called no more Jacob, but Israel," says the divine opponent, "for as a prince hast thou power with God and with men, and hast prevailed" (Gen. 32:28). Having survived the encounter with the divine, he can now venture to enter Canaan and face his brother.

The desert generation is far more confused and fearful about homecoming than the eponymous patriarch. The discontinuities, or the fissures of identity, that characterize the return of the individual hero are far more pronounced in the case of collective identity, a construct whose unity is far more difficult to maintain. The wandering Israelites are skeptical about the very premise that Canaan is their homeland. The only land they wish to return to is Egypt. But they end up in the wilderness, between Egypt and the Promised Land, returning to neither. They remain, in other words, in an in-between zone, between infancy and adulthood, in a prolonged phase of unsettled and unsettling youth. Jeremiah remembers the period of wanderings in the desert as a golden age, in which the nation followed God devotedly with a "kindness of youth" (*chesed ne'urim;* 2:2). Such "kindness," however, is shattered by moments in which the Israelites refuse to follow the Father and seek other routes.

The desire to return to Egypt is evident from the outset, but in Numbers 13 the people are ready to act on it. They seek another leader (*rosh*) who would reverse the nation's course. It is a moment of intense controversy that calls into question the official construction of Canaan as national home. To better understand the fracture, let us explore further Moses' vision of the Promised Land.

The Land of the Fathers

Moses attempts to create what is so central to the formation of national belonging: a sense of home.[4] He relies on two concepts: "the land of milk and honey" and "the land of the fathers." Home, for Moses, is a chronotope where the mother—who is revealed solely via figurative language—provides space and the fathers provide the temporal dimension. As Julia Kristeva suggests, this division is a common one: "When evoking the name and destiny of women, one thinks more of the *space* generating and forming the human species than of *time*, becoming or history."[5] The division between parental time and maternal space, however, is rather fuzzy. National time is revealed in national space and vice versa. Similarly, the paternal and maternal aspects are inextricably connected.

I will begin with the fathers. The children of Israel spend four hundred years (or four hundred thirty, according to another tradition) in Egypt oblivious to their past. It is left for Moses to evoke—or fashion—those long-forgotten memories about the three founding patriarchs, the divine Promise, and the ancient patrimony far away. Just before the Exodus, Moses addresses the children of Israel in God's name, saying:

> I am the Lord, and I will bring you out from under the burdens of the Egyptians, and I will rid you out of their bondage. . . . And I will bring you in unto the land, concerning the which I did swear to give it to Abraham, to Isaac, and to Jacob; and I will give it you for an heritage. (Exod. 6:6–8)

From the depths of misery, "from under the burdens" of bondage, God will lift them up to the land of promise, the land he swore (literally, raised His hand) to give to their ancestors, to Abraham, Isaac, and Jacob. "The nation, like the individual," Ernest Renan writes, "is the culmination of a long past of endeavors, sacrifice, and devotion. Of all cults, that of the ancestors is the most legitimate, for the ancestors made us what we are. A heroic past, great men of glory . . . this is the social capital upon which one bases a national idea."[6] Moses offers the children of Israel a respectable lineage: three fathers who had the privileged position of the chosen, who won the favor of God and were deemed worthy of a promise and a heritage. They are models to be cherished and imitated for those who wish to be counted among the chosen. To return to Canaan is thus defined as a return home, as a quest for lost roots, a continuation of the glorious lives of the three founding patriarchs.

Moses establishes "continuity with a suitable historical past," in Eric Hobsbawm's terms.[7] The promise that is given in the past is meant for the future, for the "seed" of the founding fathers, the nation to be. Much like the Trojan refugees in the *Aeneid* who discover (after a few misdiscoveries) that Italy, where they end up founding a new nation, is their ancestral home, so the Israelites discover that Canaan is their land from time immemorial.[8] Whether or not the "true origins" of the Israelites lie in Canaan, there is a significant breach of time between the patriarchs and the liberated Hebrew slaves, a breach that Moses denies as he sends spies to follow the route of their ancestors and explore the land that the latter possessed.

The Best of All Feminine Worlds

I suggested earlier that the concept of a land of milk and honey may be seen as an infantile dream of wish fulfillment, an image of a benevolent motherland whose milk is always available, flowing in abundance, intermingled with honey. The Promised Land, in other words, is imagined as a perfect mother with a perfect nature who can satisfy all the desires of the young nation: plenitude, pleasure, love, and security. One needs to bear in mind, however, that in a sense the mother is a beloved as well, something that becomes all the more evident the closer the Israelites get to Canaan. The sexual dimension of milk and honey is revealed in the Song of Songs under the tongue of the Shulamite. "Thy lips, O my spouse, drop as the honeycomb: honey and milk under thy tongue" (4:11), says the lover to his beloved while seducing her to open up her locked garden with its sealed fountain (*gan na'ul, ma'ayan chatum*). To reach the Promised Land thus means to find the best of all feminine gardens: maternal nurturing coupled with erotic delights.

Michael Walzer insists on the differences between the Promised Land and the Garden of Eden:

> Eden is a mythical garden while the promised land has latitude and longitude; Eden stands at the beginning and then, in messianic thought, at the very end of human history, while the promised land is firmly located within history; and Eden represents the perfection of nature and human nature, while the promised land is simply a better place than Egypt was.[9]

Walzer rightly criticizes the Christian presuppositions of Northrop Frye's interpretation of the Promised Land as synonymous with the Garden of Eden and ultimately with the Kingdom of God, "the home of the soul," but in doing so he overlooks the mythical qualities of the locus, the extent to which the concept of milk and honey indeed calls to mind paradisiacal landscapes of feminine plenitude.[10] Joel's prophecy regarding the end of days illuminates the utopian connotations of the metaphor: "And it shall come to pass in that day, that the mountains shall drop down new wine [the Hebrew word *'asis* also stands for fruit juice] and the hills shall flow with milk" (3:18; cf. Isa. 66:9–13). I do not wish to refute the literal aspects of Canaan or the historical thrust of the narrative but rather to show that the Promised Land, much like the nation that calls it "home," has an imaginary base.

The Startling Sight

At first sight, however, Canaan does not seem like home sweet home. It definitely does not radiate the kind of warmth and familiarity one would expect. What the spies—the ten rebellious ones—seem to claim is that the mother / bride who was to welcome them home turned out to be a great disappointment. Instead of supplying her sons and lovers with the goods, with the promised milk and honey, she threatens "to devour the inhabitants of the land" (*eretz okhelet yoshveha*). Instead of being a source of nourishment, an object of desire, she becomes a perverse mother with cannibalistic impulses and an appetite of her own.

On the paternal front the picture is not brighter. In this case the fathers, or their traces, are simply absent. Their absence is all the more threatening in light of the fact that the land is packed with other nations. "The Amalekites dwell in the land of the south," say the spies, "and the Hittites, and the Jebusites, and the Amorites, dwell in the mountains: and the Canaanites dwell by the sea, and by the coast of Jordan" (Num. 13:29). There is no empty place no matter what direction one chooses. Neither God nor Moses conceals the fact that the land of the fathers is in the possession of others, but the promise includes divine intervention against the natives. "And I will send an angel before thee; and I will drive out the Canaanite, the Amorite, and the Hittite, and the Perizzite, the Hivite, and the Jebusite" (Exod. 33:2). And yet, on seeing the inhabitants of the land, the possibility of them vanishing into thin air seemed far less plausible. The land was truly theirs. No glimpse of continuity with the patriarchal tradition was to be seen on the horizon. The only past the spies evoke is a prepatriarchal one. They depict the tall inhabitants of Canaan as *nefilim*, the legendary gigantic heroes of the antediluvian period who were considered to be the curious product of the couplings between the sons of God and the daughters of Adam (Gen. 6:2–4). The history of the patriarchs is provocatively eclipsed as another continuity between the nefilim and the inhabitants of Canaan is established. For the spies, the Promised Land is not merely an Old

World awaiting their return. It resembles a threatening—though marvelous—New World whose relation to Israelite historiography is questionable.

New Worlds: New Food

Travel accounts regarding the "discovery" of the New World can teach us much about the first encounter of the spies with the Promised Land. The relevance of the comparison did not escape William Bradford. In his report on the Pilgrims' first explorations of New England, he alludes to the story of the spies' expedition to Canaan. He writes of sixteen armed men, under the conduct of Captain Standish, who ventured to explore the shore of Cape Cod. To their delight, they discovered buried Indian baskets full of corn, which they hastened to bring back to the ship. "And so like the men of Eshcol [the cluster of grapes], carried with them of the fruits of the land and showed their brethren, of which, and their return, they were marvelously glad and their hearts encouraged."[11]

Bradford uses Scripture to legitimate their deeds and to familiarize the strange world they had discovered. I will do the opposite—that is, I will use the writings of New World discoverers to shed light on the sense of estrangement vis-à-vis the Promised Land, to highlight the "newness" of Canaan.

In *Marvelous Possessions*, Stephen Greenblatt offers a fascinating reading of the sense of wonder and anxiety that accompanied the European encounter with the New World. "Columbus's voyage," Greenblatt claims, "initiated a century of intense wonder. European culture experienced something like the 'startle reflex' one can observe in infants: eyes widened, arms overstretched, breathing stilled, the whole body momentarily convulsed."[12] And this shock at the sight of the new and unknown generated certain types of narrative. One of the characteristic features of such travel tales, as Greenblatt shows, is the tendency to denote "some departure, displacement, or surpassing of the normal or the probable."[13] Consider Columbus's account of Española: it is "very fertile to a limitless degree"; its harbors are "beyond comparison with others which I know in Christendom"; it has many good and large rivers "which is marvelous [*que es maravilla*]"; and its mountains are "most beautiful, of a thousand shapes, and all are accessible and filled with trees of a thousand kinds and tall, and they seem to touch the sky."[14]

A similar experience of wonder is evident in the spies' depiction of the exceptional fertility of Canaan, in their admiration of the new lush fruits they discovered, samples of a different agriculture and a different climate, unknown back in the irrigated flat lands of Egypt.[15] Here too nature is beyond measure, particularly the grapes. Two men are needed to carry one cluster. And then, of course, there is the interminable flow of milk and honey. The surpassing of measure includes the inhabitants of the land as well. Three different terms are used to underline the unusual stature of the men they encountered: *'anshey midot* (men of great stature), *bnei 'anak* (sons of giants), and *nefilim* (the primordial gigantic heroes). And as if all these synonyms were not enough, they go on to explain, "We were in our own sight as grasshoppers, and so we were in their sight" (Num. 13:33).

The spies' words disclose the projection at work. They move swiftly from their perspective to that of the giants, never considering the possibility that the latter may have a different worldview. The midrash already noted the phenomenon when conjecturing God's response to the spies: "I take no objection to your saying 'We looked like grasshoppers to ourselves' but I take offense when you say 'so we must have looked to them.' How do you know how I made you look to them? Perhaps you appeared to them as angels?"[16]

The shock at the sight of the other and the fantasies and projections created as a result are a familiar feature in European descriptions of the natives of the New World. The natives were often depicted as utterly strange in their appearance and customs. The most powerful fantasy, however, operative in all early encounters in the New World, was cannibalism. In part, it was a matter of misinterpreting different eating habits and unfamiliar non-Christian religious rituals, but it also had to do with a more primary anxiety about losing one's identity in the other. As Greenblatt suggests, "The Spaniards' greatest fear was that they would be assimilated, literally absorbed, by being eaten."[17]

The fear of cannibalism hovers over the travel account of the spies as well. The land as a whole is described as a cannibalistic (m)other who swallows up her children. And even the representation of the giants is colored in similar hues insofar as grasshoppers are known as the smallest edible animal according to biblical law (see Lev. 11:22).

There are significant differences between the biblical explorers and the "discoverers" of the New World. In the account of the spies, unlike Columbus's *Diario*, there is more fear than wonder, although in both cases one finds an intriguing mixture of the two. Whereas Columbus, Cortés, and the American Pilgrims seize the lands they explore ravenously, the spies—who perceive themselves as inferior in size and power to the natives—recommend avoiding the conquest of Canaan. Bradford surely smooths out the subversive aspect of the tale in contriving a "happy ending" to the story. According to his narrative, Captain Standish and his men return from the shore with the fruits of the land (the corn) and all were "marvelously glad" and much "encouraged." But the biblical spies are neither encouraged nor encouraging. They come to uncover the secrets of the land, to uncover "her nakedness," to use Joseph's definition of spying (on accusing his brothers of spying on Egypt), but are overwhelmed by the sight.[18]

Unheimlich

In "The Uncanny," Freud points to the curious phenomenon of the fragile demarcation between what is *heimlich* (familiar, belonging to home) and what is *unheimlich* (unfamiliar, strange, dreadful—uncanny). The demarcation is fragile to the extent that *heimlich* at times means *unheimlich* under the sign of repression. Let me suggest that a similar collapse of boundaries takes place in Numbers 13. Canaan is more than a strange New World: it is a haunted, alienated home. The mother's body is one of Freud's famous examples for the feeling of (un)heimlich:

> There is a humorous saying, "Love is homesickness"; and whenever a man dreams of a place or a country and says to himself, still in the dream, "this place is familiar to me, I have been here before," we may interpret the place as being his mother's genitals or her body. In this case, too, the *unheimlich* is what was once *heimisch*, home-like, familiar; the prefix "un" is the token of repression.[19]

The spies' expedition may be construed as the opposite dream. They say to themselves: "this place is unfamiliar to us, we have never been here before." But given the fluidity of (un)heimlich, the underlying message of their narrative is similar. The Promised Land is envisioned as the body of an estranged mother; it is an unheimlich that was once heimisch, or rather remembered as such.[20]

The giants too are part of this uncanny scene. Strangely enough, there is something familiar about them: they seem to represent not only the indigenous Canaanite population but also a distorted image of the patriarchs. The fathers and the others blend at points. The fact that the giants turn up, of all places, in the area of Hebron, the burial site of Abraham, Isaac, and Jacob (see Gen. 23), reinforces this notion, as if they were tall ghosts of the distant forefathers, who have risen from their grave in the cave of Machpela to haunt their descendants.[21] Note that the term *refa'im*, associated with the giants of Hebron in Deuteronomy 2:11, makes an analogous connection: it stands both for a legendary pre-Israelite community in Canaan and for the ghosts of the underworld.[22] Canaan, far more than Egypt, seems, from the spies' point of view, a shadowy, frightful realm, dominated by the dead. Voyages to the underworld to speak with the dead (of the kind found in *The Epic of Gilgamesh* or in the *Odyssey*) are impossible within the biblical framework, where Sheol remains a secluded realm below, beyond narrative, but at times mythical overtones seep into the text, hinting at a more dramatic underworld behind the scenes.

Bruno Bettelheim's work on fairy tales may shed further light on the role of the giants. According to Bettelheim, giants usually stand for adults, and more often for fathers, which is why children take so much pleasure in seeing the big creatures being fooled by their small heroes. This, of course, is not the case in our tale. What the spies sense on seeing the giants is primarily powerlessness.

They seem to shudder at the thought that they will never "grow up" or reach such stature. The tradition Moses had invented for them has a dark side. If they really had such glorious ancestors, how could they follow in their footsteps? Canaan is the land of the "grown-ups," which means that there is no room in it for them. But then their reluctance to enter the world of adults is also a challenge to the underlying presuppositions of adulthood. Adulthood entails conquest and a mode of heroism they find hard to accept.

The Revised Version

In Joshua 2 we are given a revision of Numbers 13 that accentuates the antithetical character of the first expedition to Canaan. Joshua sends two spies to explore Jericho before approaching his first target in Canaan. Joshua, as one recalls, supported the official line already in Numbers. It is he and Caleb who inverted the claim of the other ten spies in describing the inhabitants of Canaan as "bread" (Num 14:9) that can be eaten up easily. And indeed, forty years later, Joshua sets out to "devour" the Promised Land and force the cannibalistic mother back to her position as an object of desire, whose only role is to provide her hungry children with the milk and honey they long for.

Joshua's spies reach Jericho and lodge in the house of the prostitute Rahab. The king of Jericho tries to catch them, but Rahab hides them in the roof of the house, explaining her motives to the men at length:

> I know that the Lord hath given you the land, and that your terror is fallen upon us, and that all the inhabitants of the land faint because of you. For we have heard how the Lord

> dried up the water of the Red Sea for you, when ye came out of Egypt. (Josh. 2:9–10)

Rahab goes on to request that once they conquer the city they will not harm her family. The giants have disappeared and so has the mythical aroma. This time it is not the spies whose hearts fall at the sight of the inhabitants but rather the natives who "faint" at the prospects of an Israelite invasion: a significant departure from the previous tale.

Rahab is a key figure in the drama. Her theophoric name, which means "God has broadened," or "God will broaden" (like the name "Rehavia"), intimates that she serves as an opening of sorts, a gate to the Promised Land.[23] Put differently, Rahab, who resides at the city wall, points to the way in which the "fortified cities" of Canaan may be penetrated. With the scarlet rope that she ties as a sign on her window (the same rope with which she helped the two spies escape), she makes clear that Jericho, like the other cities of Canaan, is not as impenetrable as it may seem at first sight. There is a breach in the wall and a hopeful red rope in the window.[24]

Rahab plays a role similar to that of Doña Marina, La Malinche, in the conquest of Mexico. Doña Marina, the daughter of Aztec lords, served as both mistress of and translator for Cortés. In addition to her outstanding linguistic ability, she had an acute understanding of Mesoamerican reality and the capacity to make Cortés grasp it. The question of difference in language is ignored in the context of the conquest of Canaan, but here too there was an urgent need for a competent interpreter. Much like Doña Marina, Rahab is an agent of communication.[25] She provides the two spies with invaluable strategic information regarding how the Israelites are actually perceived by the other.[26] It is no longer a matter of projection. And yet her voice does not only represent the discourse of the other. She "quotes" key phrases from the Song of the Sea—"Then the dukes of Edom shall be amazed; the mighty men of Moab, trembling shall take hold upon them; all the inhabitants of Canaan shall melt away" (Exod. 15:15)—translating the perspective of the inhabitants of Canaan into familiar biblical expressions.[27]

What is more, the spies, like Cortés, lie with their informer. The conquest of the land goes hand in hand with sexual conquest. The biblical text does not offer a detailed description of the affair; it is simply intimated via the word *lie*, which means both "to lodge" and "to have sexual relations." While the spies in Numbers merely pluck the fruit but do not eat it (and the sexual connotations of fruit eating are all too well known from the days of Eden), in Joshua 2 the situation is quite different. The nation is "mature" enough to conquer. The people do not shy away from sexuality or from possessing the land; they are willing to break through the fortified virginal walls of Jericho and demand their patrimony. But let us return to the wilderness, to the moment of rupture in national historiography.

The Question of Heroism

The desert generation, unlike Joshua and his men, is not a generation of warriors. On hearing the spies' report, the people lift up their voice and cry.

> And the people wept that night. And all the children of Israel murmured against Moses and against Aaron: and the whole congregation said unto them, Would God that we had died

> in the land of Egypt! or would God we had died in this wilderness! And wherefore hath the Lord brought us unto this land, to fall by the sword, that our wives and our children should be a prey? were it not better for us to return into Egypt? And they said one to another, Let us make a captain, and let us return into Egypt. (Num. 14:1–4)

The topic of complaints this time is the Promised Land. To settle in Canaan means to engage in war, and war means "falling by the sword"—something that has no charm whatsoever as far as they are concerned. Heroism in the conventional sense is rejected shamelessly. Fighting with giants, as Don Quixote reminds us, is the dream of every warrior (David, who managed to triumph over the giant Goliath, is exemplary in this connection)—but the wandering Israelites do not find such dreams attractive. They worry about the horrifying outcome of war, the possibility that their wives will be captured and their children be as prey in the hands of the enemy. They refuse to endanger their lives. While Moses insists that there is no other home but Canaan, the desert generation wonders as to the validity and value of the newly discovered memories of the Promised Land. And wondering means wandering—being in exile.

Carcasses in the Wilderness

God's response is harsh. He is tired of their complaints. "Ten times" they have "tried" Him and He cannot take it any longer (Num. 14:22). First they rejected His laws, then His manna, and now the land He had designated for them. Once again, as in the episode of the Golden Calf, God is ready to annihilate the nation on the spot and fashion another via Moses, but Moses manages to dissuade Him. And yet the pardon is only partial. The people are by no means exempt from punishment. In His wrath, God chooses to take their request literally:

> Say unto them, As truly as I live, saith the Lord, as ye have spoken in mine ears, so will I do to you: Your carcases shall fall in this wilderness; and all that were numbered of you, according to your whole number, from twenty years old and upward, which have murmured against me, Doubtless ye shall not come into the land, concerning which I sware to make you dwell therein, save Caleb the son of Jephuneh, and Joshua the son of Nun. But your little ones, which ye said should be a prey, them will I bring in, and they shall know the land which ye have despised. But as for you, your carcases, they shall fall in this wilderness. And your children shall wander in the wilderness forty years, and bear your whoredoms, until your carcases be wasted in the wilderness. (Num. 14:28–33)

Given that dying in the wilderness seemed preferable to them than waging war on the Canaanites, He'll grant them their wish. They will die in the wilderness, not immediately, but within forty years of wanderings. The depiction of their death is blunt and gruesome. It sounds like an elaborate sonorous curse, voiced repeatedly. They will not simply die in the desert but rather "drop dead," or in biblical idiom, their "carcases will fall," with nothing to soften the blow, without, one suspects, the elementary right of the dead: burial.[28] Instead of going up to Canaan, they will fall as low as one can get. Their death will be total, their bodies will be wasted completely (*'ad tom pigrekhem*) in the arid desert, leaving no room to hope for a change of fate. The Promised Land will remain forever beyond their reach.

The children of the desert generation, however, the very children they feared would fall prey, will ultimately enter Canaan and settle there. While the parents are doomed to "know" what it means to thwart God (Num. 14:34), their offspring will have the privilege to "know" the Promised Land.[29] Their only suffering will be caused not by God but by the burden of their parents' "whoredoms," which they will need to bear for many years until the carcasses of the desert generation fall apart, setting them free.

The Cluster of Grapes: New Sites on an Old Map

Greek mythology tells of Persephone, Demeter's daughter, who yielded to Hades' offer and took a few seeds of pomegranate on leaving him. As a result, she was doomed to return every year to the underworld for four months. Something similar happens to the spies. In picking the fruit of the Promised Land, they become part of it, regardless of their fears and reservations. According to a parenthetical comment of the narrator, we learn that the place where they had found the fruit "was called the brook of Eshcol [cluster], because of the cluster of grapes which the children of Israel cut down from thence" (Num. 13:24).

Naming is a mode of discursive appropriation that is an integral part of every conquest.[30] The conquest of Canaan is no exception. When Joshua crosses the Jordan (in an act that is modeled on the crossing of the Red Sea), on the way to Jericho, he performs a naming ceremony. Twelve stones are taken from the Jordan River and placed together as a monument to commemorate the occasion of the entrance of the twelve tribes to Canaan.

At this symbolic site all the men are circumcised together by means of sharp knives made of flint (circumcision was apparently not practiced in the wilderness). Joshua chooses to call the place Gilgal, and God provides the explanation: "This day have I rolled away [*galoti*] the reproach of Egypt from off you" (Josh. 5:9). The pun on which this naming speech relies associates the name Gilgal with the root *glh*. The cutting of the foreskin, on the threshold of Canaan, is seen as God's rolling off the disgrace of Egypt, the turning of a new national page, far away from the humiliation of bondage. And yet Canaan, unlike America, is not treated as a blank page.[31] To be sure, Canaanite history is indeed effaced, much as Native American names were wiped off the map, but at the same time older names, or names that are construed as old, are retrieved. What the returning Israelites wish to do is to add new sites to the old map of the patriarchs.

The spies are not the agents of naming; it is not they who call the brook Eshcol. And yet their story participates in the appropriation of Canaan. In taking the fruit, they commit themselves to the land of milk and honey and disclose their underlying desire to conquer it, to taste its fruits, to make new marks on the ancestral map: to imprint the name "Eshcol" alongside "Hebron," the burial site of the patriarchs.

The desert generation, despite itself, craves for a home of its own, free of oppression and shame. The people yearn for it to the extent that right after the conflict over the spies' report, they regret having rejected Canaan and decide to wage war against the Amalekites and the Canaanites: "And they rose up early in the morning, and gat them up into the top of the mountain, saying, Lo, we be here, and will go up [*hinenu ve'alinu*] unto the place which the Lord hath promised: for we have sinned" (Num. 14:40).

Now they finally want to go up the mountain and seek the promise, but it is too late. Moses warns them that because of their sin God will not stand by them in battle. They insist on trying. As expected, they lose. The Amalekites and the Canaanites who dwell in that hill come down and smite them (14:45). It is an aborted attempt to climb up the mountain that marks their ongoing ambivalence with respect to Canaan.

The Desert Generation

The desert generation has been regarded in diverse ways by commentators. Abraham Ibn Ezra, among others, accuses the members of this generation of having a slave mentality that did not allow them to enjoy their freedom or to stand up against their enemies. Having internalized the Pharaonic attitude toward them, they cannot perceive themselves as other than inferior. Such interpretations fail to take account of the power embedded in their rebellion against God and the audacity evident in their challenge to national dreams.

The Talmud offers a different interpretive route in its fascinating representation of the grandeur of the desert's Dead. Rabbah b. Bar Hana relates a story he had heard from a traveling Arab:

> Come and I will show you the Dead of the Wilderness. I went [with him] and saw them; and they looked as if in a state of exhilaration. They slept on their backs; and the knee of one of them was raised, and the Arab merchant passed under the knee riding on a camel with a spear erect, and did not touch it. I cut off one corner of the purple blue shawl of one of them; and we could not move away. He said unto me:

> [if] you have, peradventure, taken something from them, return it; for we have a tradition that he who takes anything from them cannot move away. I went and returned it; and then we were able to move away.[32]

The talmudic reading is well aware of the vitality of the struggle of the desert generation and the stature of its tragic death. The carcasses of the Dead of the wilderness, according to this tradition, did not fall apart but miraculously survived the erosive forces of nature and became part of the desert landscape. Indeed, they may be found intact in the arid land, for their resilience is so great that no one could harm them, or even cut a single corner of their shawl without being paralyzed. The most remarkable detail of this reading, however, is the gigantic measure of the Dead. The merchant who passes under the knee of one of them with a spear is incapable of touching it. The grasshoppers, strangely enough, turn into awe-inspiring desert giants.

Bialik, the major poet of the Hebrew renaissance, uses this talmudic legend as an epigraph to his remarkable poem, "The Dead of the Desert." Following the ancient legend, he depicts the vital dead as giants who "lie stretched in the sun, beside their dark pavilions, on the yellow dunes of the desert, in lion-like somnolence."[33] What he adds to the talmudic source is a momentous, almost mythical, struggle of the desert generation against the Creator. At times, we are told, the dead rise from their eternal sleep to rebel in a desert storm against the divine hand that imprisoned them in the desolate waste.

> We are the brave!
> Last of the enslaved!

First to be free!
With our strong hand,
our hand alone,
we tore from our neck
the heavy yoke.
Raised our heads to the skies,
narrowed them with our eyes.
Renegades of the waste,
we called barrenness mother. . . .
In the desert imprisoned,
to misery abandoned
by an avenging God,
a mere whispered song
of defiance and revolt
stirred us to rise. . . .
The storm calls: Dare!
Take lance, take spear.
Let the mountains break up,
the hills collapse,
or our bodies lie heaped
corpse upon corpse.
Onwards to the hills
arise, ascend [*hinene ve'alinu*]![34]

Bialik interprets the people's attempt to go up the mountain and wage war despite Moses' admonition in Numbers 14 as their ultimate rebellion against the cruel punishment inflicted on them. They refuse to be wasted in the wilderness. They have the unique power of a people who are "the last of the enslaved" and "the first to be free," ready to protest against any mode of enslavement—

whether by Pharaoh or by God. It is a generation that was born via a struggle with God and dies in a forceful struggle against Him. In a sense they stand for the nation as a whole, whose name, from the outset, foretells a history of wrestlings with the Father.

The spirit of the desert generation unsettles future generations as well. Even when the Israelites finally invade Canaan, the wandering does not fully stop. Exile piles up on exile. The Promised Land throughout biblical times is regarded with a certain degree of ambivalence.[35] It is never seen as truly a stable home, or as the only center of holiness. "I remember thee, the kindness of thy youth, the love of thine espousals, when thou wentest after me in the wilderness, in a land that was not sown," says Jeremiah in the name of God to Israel (2 : 2). In this passage Jeremiah ventures to claim that the desert offers a youthful passion the Promised Land lacks. He realizes with his wandering precursors that a land that is not "sown" leaves more room for dreaming than a tilled land. Settling down, like "growing up," has its disadvantages.

Despite its antinational tendencies, the desert generation became a legendary generation of national ancestors. The narrative of Exodus-Numbers has tremendous resonance in the Bible itself (far more than the Book of Joshua), not to mention later commentary. Biblical historiography points to the complexity of national imagination. Powerful national narratives are not necessarily based on idealized epic renditions of devoted ancestors who had no qualms, nor are they based strictly on laudatory depictions of the homeland's terrain. The Promised Land is at the same time a land of milk and honey and a land that devours its inhabitants.

A Final Glimpse

Exile makes clear that every construction of home is arbitrary. Home is where one wants to be, the imagined locus one yearns for from afar. In the following episode in Numbers 16 Moses is challenged once again, this time by Dathan and Aviram, who ask: "Is it a small thing that thou hast brought us up out of a land that floweth with milk and honey, to kill us in the wilderness, except thou make thyself altogether a prince over us?" (16:13). They provocatively turn *Egypt* into the land that flows with milk and honey, calling into question Moses' authority and national vision. Their punishment is not without significance: the earth of the desert "opens her mouth" and swallows them up. They go down alive "into Sheol," the realm of the dead (16:30). Canaan is not inherently a land of milk and honey, nor is it the only land with cannibalistic tendencies. Any land can be both. Any land can be both the home of the living and the home of the dead. It all depends on the eye of the spy.

CHAPTER SIX

Crossing the Threshold

In the Plains of Moab

Israel approaches the threshold of the Promised Land once again after some forty years of roaming and discovers various guardians on Canaan's borders—the neighboring nations of Transjordan—that complicate the passage into the ancestral home. Edom is the first to block the entrance. Moses sends messengers to the king of Edom from Kadesh, asking for permission to use the king's road on the way to Canaan, though he does not dare evoke the name of their final destination: "Thus saith thy brother Israel.... Let us pass, I pray thee, through thy country: we will not pass through the fields, or through the vineyards, neither will we drink of the water of the wells: we will go by the king's high way... until we have passed thy borders" (Num. 20:14–17). But Edom refuses to let Israel pass through and threatens to use force if necessary to bar the way. More than literal rights of passage are at stake. To let Israel pass through means to acknowledge its right to inherit, to possess land, to pass from the position of the son to that of the father, to become an established nation despite its belated birth. The struggle between Jacob and Esau over the patrimony is reenacted in national terms. Moses, indeed, evokes the primary negotiations between the eponymous ancestors in addressing Edom as Israel's "brother."[1] Invoking kinship, however, is of no avail, nor are the painful recollections of Israel's bondage in Egypt that Moses adds to his plea. Edom is unwilling to welcome his young sibling back home. The king's road is shut. It takes another detour—around the land of Edom—before the Israelites are ready to insist on their right to pass through. This time they send messengers to Sihon, the king of Amor, and when the latter turns down their request for passage they wage war against him and conquer the land of the Amorites. The land of Bashan is conquered shortly after. Israel's entry to the Promised Land now seems certain, but military success apparently does not suffice, for another station is required before Israel can pass through and take possession of its inheritance. The last station on the winding route of the wanderings is situated on the bank of the Jordan River, facing Jericho: the plains of Moab.

Much narrative space is allotted to the plains of Moab—from the final chapters of Numbers (22–36) through the entire book of Deuteronomy and the first two chapters of Joshua—though Israel spent but a few months there. The lengthy treatment of this last station points to the importance of the site as well as to the difficulties embedded in the transition to national adulthood.[2] The people now have more power than ever before, and the land is almost within reach: it lies right there on the other bank of the Jordan, no longer a remote dream. Jericho, the first city to be conquered in Canaan, can already be seen on the horizon. And yet liminal anxieties hover in the air: Is Israel truly mature enough, worthy enough, to cross over?

Such anxieties call for a rite that would ease the dangerous and demanding leap. Let me suggest that an extended, if fragmentary, initiation rite takes place in this liminal station, beginning with the blessings of Balaam and ending with the nation's ceremonial crossing of the Jordan under the leadership of Joshua. The momentous rite at Mount Sinai was a primary and unparalleled moment of initiation, in which God revealed Himself and His writings to the nation. Initiation, however, does not end on the threshold of adolescence. Crossing the threshold of adulthood—becoming the people of the Land (not only the people of the Book)—requires another rebirth, another revelatory moment, another ritual process, additional sets of laws, and different imaginings.

I focus here on the treatment of this last station in the final chapters of Numbers. Deuteronomy—where Moses retells the nation's history in the course of renewing the covenant of Sinai—as well as the account in Joshua of the actual crossing remain beyond the scope of this book. I show that the key stories of the plains of Moab in Numbers—Balaam, the affair of Baal Peor, the census, the apportionment of land, and the war against Midian—are all inextricably connected in their attempt to define the initiatory character of this liminal zone. What the account in Numbers underlines is the complication of an initiation that is set against the first encounter with Canaanite culture. The wilderness offered a cultural lacuna of sorts. But that intimate guarded seclusion with God—far away from other peoples and other deities in an "empty howling waste" (though never totally empty)—comes to an end as the Israelites camp in the plains of Moab, meet the local inhabitants, and discover their religious customs.

The plains of Moab call to mind what Bhabha terms the inbetween, the zone of intersection in which all culturally determinate significations are challenged by an unresolved and unresolvable hybridity. It is an unstable and unpredictable zone, where the boundaries between Israel and its neighbors are constructed and blurred repeatedly, providing "overwhelming evidence of a more transnational and translational sense of the hybridity of imagined communities."[3]

Mircea Eliade's notion of initiation as entrance into a coherent cultural framework—a rite through which the initiate is introduced into "the whole body of the tribe's mythological and cultural traditions"—does not hold in this case.[4] What we have on the threshold of the Promised Land is a "cross-cultural initiation" that relies extensively on a cultural exchange with the other—so much so that the one who plays the opening role in initiating the nation into the mysteries of adulthood is not Moses but rather a foreign seer: Balaam, the son of Beor.[5]

Balak, Balaam, and the Ass: A Cultural Trial of Strength

The story of Balaam in Numbers 22–24, the first episode in the plains of Moab, stands out in its rather unusual style: an intriguing patchwork of folkloric-carnivalesque narrative and sections of exquisite poetic blessings.[6] Balaam's blessings convey the most distinct initiatory note in this context, but what precedes them is no less important. The tale begins with the very opposite of a blessing: the threat of a curse. It begins with culture wars between Israel and Moab: Whose culture shall prevail? Who has control over language, the power to bless or to curse? The encounter with the other's culture is by no means devoid of tension.

Seeing the fearful fate of Amor and Bashan, Balak, king of Moab, decides to put a hex on the Israelites that will hinder their advance and drive them out of the land. He summons Balaam, the renowned pagan seer, who is something of a magician, to curse Israel on his behalf. "Behold," he says,

> there is a people come out from Egypt: behold, they cover the face [lit., the eye] of the earth, and they abide over against me: Come now therefore, I pray thee, curse me this people; for they are too mighty for me: peradventure I shall prevail, that we may smite them . . . for I wot that he whom thou blessest is blessed, and he whom thou cursest is cursed. (22:5–6)

Like Pharaoh, Balak is threatened (*va-yakots mi-penei*) by the large numbers of Israelites and regards them as too numerous and mighty (*'atsum*) for him (cf. Exod. 1:9, 1:12).[7] But then there are noticeable differences. Israel is no longer a community of slaves under the rule of another nation: it has "come out of Egypt" and has the force to "lick up" whatever stands in its way. Balak's only hope is that magic—of the best quality—will enable him to overcome the potential invaders, whose appetite is as big as that of an ox (Num. 22:4) or swarms of locusts covering "the eye of the earth."[8]

To Balak's great dismay, however, Balaam does not use his legendary power to curse Israel but rather blesses the rising nation—in a carnivalesque twist—time and again. Monotheism truimphs. Even the greatest pagan seer discovers the grandeur of God and Israel. But this triumph requires a struggle. Balaam does not easily yield to God's command, and even when he follows divine orders there is an element of resistance in his stance. He oscillates between Balak and God, between cursing and blessing, between sorcery and prophecy. God first addresses Balaam in a dream shortly after Balak's emissaries summon him. "Thou shalt not go with them," God says to Balaam, "thou shalt not curse the people: for they are blessed" (22:12). Balaam at first seems to comply with God's demand as he refuses to join the Moabite dignitaries. But then he welcomes the second delegation, "more numerous and distinguished than the first," asking them to remain overnight, hoping that God will deliver a different message.

God finally sends Balaam off to Balak, but the journey is not devoid of obstacles. An angel turns up in his way as an adversary. Balaam's ass—one of the earliest specimens of the comic folkloric ass—shies away from the sword-brandishing angel and turns aside.[9] Balaam, who is blind to the presence of God's messenger, beats her furiously, in an attempt to direct her back to the path. The angel, however, is still around. On seeing him in the narrow path between the vineyards, the ass thrusts herself against the fence and crushes Balaam's foot. She is beaten again. Finally, in the most astonishing moment of the tale, after realizing that there is no way to escape the angel, the ass collapses, falls down under Balaam, and wondrously opens her mouth (with the exception of the serpent in the Garden of Eden, animals are not granted the gift of speech in biblical narrative): "What have I done unto thee, that thou hast smitten me these three times. . . . Am not I thine ass, upon which thou hast ridden ever since I was thine unto this day?" (22:28–30). The wise beast rebukes Balaam in human speech, making an ass of her master, forcing him to see the angel that stands before his eyes, blocking the passage. And if this weren't humiliating enough for the seer, the angel reinforces the ass's words and hails her sharp vision: "And the ass saw me, and turned from me these three times: unless she had turned from me, surely now also I had slain thee, and saved her alive" (22:33). Only at this point does Balaam acknowledge his blindness and become God's agent.

Eyes Unveiled: Revelation from the Bottom Up

The humorous juxtaposition of the ass and Balaam serves in part to ridicule the renowned pagan seer whose ass is more insightful than he is.[10] But the mysterious opening of the ass's mouth discloses another message: revelation comes in unexpected ways from unexpected sources—not only in the form of a fire at the top of Mount Sinai but also via the mouth of an ass. The analogy between the ass and Balaam thus entails a more complex treatment of the power relations between self and other. Just as the ass can open Balaam's eyes, so can the seer's visionary blessings unexpectedly offer an insightful comment on the state of the Israelite community.

Balaam begins his journey as a laughable fool, awkwardly unaware of his moves, but gradually turns into an admirable and inspiring seer, who can see and say what no one else in the community can—not even Moses. Leaving divination and magic behind, Balaam celebrates the pleasures of "knowing the most High," of seeing divine visions (*machaze shaday yecheze*) with "eyes unveiled" (*geluy einayim*) (Num. 24:4). Vision is not to be taken for granted; it is a divine gift that entails the lifting of a veil, the uncovering of an inner eye. Following the encounter with the angel, Balaam is endowed with the capacity to see what lies before his eyes as well as distant sights of days to come. With such visionary power, he sets out to remove some of the obstacles blocking the nation's path.[11]

Balaam's Nationscapes

Balaam's blessings are delivered in the course of burnt offerings at three different mountaintops. The construction of seven altars and the sacrifice of bulls and rams are recorded time and again. But the climactic moment of the ritual at each site is a poetic oracle that bears the power of a blessing bestowed from above:

> How can I damn whom God has not damned,
> How doom when the Lord has not doomed?
> As I see them from the mountain tops,
> Gaze on them from the heights,
> There is a people that dwells apart,
> Not reckoned among the nations,
> Who can count the dust of Jacob,
> Number the dust-cloud of Israel?
>
> (Num. 23:8–10)[12]

The first oracle displays Balaam's position. He is an outsider, an observer who stands on the tops of rocks (*rosh tsurim*), and has the advantage of seeing the children of Israel from a point to which they have no access. Israel, he proclaims, cannot be doomed. The view of the Israelites from the heights attests beyond doubt that they are blessed. Set apart, countless as the dust (in keeping with Abraham's memorable vision), they bear the mark of those chosen by God. Israel's capacity to "dwell apart, not reckoned by the nations," is seen as proof of its cultural strength. Supposedly, the problems that arose with the separation from Egypt have been resolved by now. The nation is fully formed and is no longer vulnerable to other influences, nor does it depend on the customs of others.

Balaam holds a mirror up to Israel that allows it to discover and thus constitute itself. Balak insisted that Balaam view the Israelite camp while cursing it presumably to add the power of the "evil eye" to his words. But the king's wish is inverted as Balaam's eye turns out to be a "good" eye that notes Israel's maturity and approves of it with much enthusiasm.

In the next two oracles, Balaam goes on to provide a set of epic similes that liken the chosen nation to animals of prey, underlining Israel's virility and potential for conquest.[13] Even after conquering Sihon, Israel does not seem to fully realize the extent of its powers. Curiously, instead of singing a victory song of their own, a song of another battle—the victory of Sihon over Moab—is quoted: "Woe to thee, Moab! thou art undone, O people of Chemosh: he hath given his sons that escaped, and his daughters, into captivity unto Sihon king of the Amorites" (21:29). To be sure, the song foretells implicitly that the Moabites have good reasons to fear Israel given the fact that the Israelites succeeded in overcoming Sihon, who had defeated Moab. But this citation may also intimate that Israel does not yet perceive itself as a conqueror. Victory songs are construed as the genre of others.

Balaam changes this notion by introducing Israel into the poetic framework of heroic life. Whereas Balak used a rather "herbivorous" and domestic image of an ox "licking up" the grass of the field (22:4), Balaam evokes the wild and majestic force of the lion, a classic metaphor for warriors: "Behold, the people shall rise up as a great lion, and lift up himself as a young lion: he shall not lie down until he eat of the prey, and drink the blood of the slain" (23:24).[14] The wild ox has similar capacities, for it "shall eat up the nations his enemies, and shall break their bones, and pierce them through with his arrows" (24:8–9). Israel now has teeth,

Balaam seems to claim; it has the desire to devour and crush other nations and the power to do so. The depiction of the predatory animals is vivid and gory. They are represented in a moment of action. The lion rises from crouching, lifting itself up to eat of the prey and drink of the blood, and the wild ox consumes its enemies thoroughly, to the point of crushing their bones. Military terms are inserted to highlight the analogy between the animal kingdom and the world of battle. The blood the lion thrives on is the blood of the slain—*chalalim*, a term that is primarily used to depict human casualties in war—and the ox's bone breaking is likened to the smashing of arrows.

The seer goes so far as suggesting that Israel's position as warrior touches on the divine. There is a metaphoric slippage at points where the same predatory animals are used to represent both the nation and God: "God who freed them from Egypt / Is for them like the horns of the wild ox" (23:22).[15] If at the crossing of the Red Sea God alone took on the position of a warrior, now the nation as a whole is mature enough to join Him and partake of the Father's glory.

The envisioned national prosperity calls for a profusion of metaphors. Similes that pertain to the animal kingdom and wars intermingle with the peaceful imagery of water and vegetation:

> How fair are your tents, O Jacob,
> Your dwellings, O Israel!
> Like palm-groves that stretch out,
> Like gardens beside a river,
> Like aloes planted by the Lord,
> Like cedars beside the water;

Their boughs drip with moisture,
Their roots [lit., seed] have abundant water.
(24:5–7)[16]

After the interminable thirst that characterized Israel's wanderings in the desert, Balaam's vision is utterly refreshing. Its point of departure is a liminal setting of comely tents, but the seer goes beyond the present moment and announces the rise of a new landscape, a secure and fertile agrarian world, where water flows both from above and from below and seeds, like roots, are drenched in "many waters." Is this a variation on the concept of a land that flows with milk and honey? Here too one can discern a mythical quality. Balaam's drenched gardens echo the Garden of Eden, planted by God near a plentiful river (Gen. 2:8–10), as well as the sensuous gardens of the lovers in the Song of Songs, where aloes (*'ahalim*), sweet-smelling trees whose sap is used as perfume, grow by fountains of "living water" (4:14–15).[17]

The unusual choice of "seed" instead of roots (smoothed over by the above translation) in the depiction of the saturated cedars suggests that the envisioned fertility will include the human realm as well (*zera* also stands for "offspring" and "semen"). The virility of the nation will thus manifest itself not only through military strength but also in sexual ripeness and procreation. "He is majestic as Lebanon / Stately as the cedars (*bachur ka'arazim*)," claims the beloved in the Song of Songs (5:15) as she enumerates the delightful qualities of her lover's body.[18] Israel too—for once at least—is represented as desirable a match as the *bachur*, the young man, of the Song of Songs.

Balaam maps out the new life that awaits the nation now that it has come of age. The Israelites are ripe for a land of their own, Balaam promises, and will thrive on taking root there. But however powerful blessings may be, they cannot guarantee a future without problems or blemishes. There are significant discrepancies between Balaam's visions and the disorderly character of historical events.

The Baal Peor Affair: Sexual Maturity and Idolatry

In the plains of Moab, as on Mount Sinai, initiatory rites are constructed and deconstructed at a dazzling pace.[19] A sharp turn of events, accompanied by a change of tone, follows Balaam's ceremonial blessing of the nation. The carnivalesque and euphoric spirit of the previous episode is replaced by a solemn laconic narrative on the nation's apostasy. The seer's perception of Israel as set apart from other nations turns out to be something of an idealization. Forbidden sexual drives erupt all of a sudden, unsettling cultural boundaries. In Numbers 25:1 we are told that the people "began to commit whoredom with the daughters of Moab." Yielding to the seduction of the Moabite women who offered them sacrificial meals, the Israelites "clung" (*va-yitsamed*—the singular masculine mode of the verb is used) unto another god, Baal Peor.[20]

This is the first time the nation's sexual conduct is dealt with explicitly—it is merely intimated in the story of the Golden Calf.[21] What this episode makes clear is that adulthood does not necessarily lead to righteous behavior. The sexual maturity of the nation is expressed in forbidden ways: whoredom and its theological correlate, idolatry. "Whereas the Golden Calf had been intended to honor YHWH," writes James Ackerman, "no such pretense is maintained with Baal Peor."[22] At the fringes of agrarian civilization, just before settling down, the Israelites encounter the fertility rain god, Baal, who seems to them a necessary addition to life beyond the desert.[23] It is no longer a question of repressed memories of a lost cultural past that erupt in the midst of a cultural lacuna but rather a scene of full-blown cultural intermingling between two peoples.

Ezekiel provides a similar narrative regarding the consequences of sexual ripeness for Jerusalem, although in this case feminine maturation is at stake. According to Ezekiel, once the foundling nation whom God had adopted and then betrothed began to bear the marks of womanhood—"thy breasts are fashioned, and thine hair is grown" (16:7)—she lacked the power to regulate her sexual drives and "whored" after other gods. The precious gifts endowed to her by God were perversely spent on her new lovers. "And of thy garments thou didst take, and deckedst thy high places with divers colours, and playedst the harlot thereupon" (16:16).[24]

In Numbers God is primarily a Father and Israel a male character, whereas in Ezekiel God is primarily a Husband and Israel a female, but in both cases God is jealous and the nation "whores" (*znh*).[25] What is more, in both cases one finds an interesting blending of roles. Ezekiel offers an explicit combination of God's paternal and amorous qualities. In the plains of Moab, the mixture is more subtle. God is represented as a Father whose ungrateful son betrays Him on growing up, not only by choosing inappropriate female mates, but also in adhering to the abominable "father-in-law," Baal, who—given the pointed sexual innuendos of the term "clung"—is something of a lover as well.[26] Mixed roles appear in the human realm as well. If Jerusalem assumes a traditional male role in courting her lovers, in Numbers one finds the opposite phenomenon. The nation's virility—just praised by Balaam—is called into question, for the potential conqueror is ironically conquered both in body and in spirit by foreign women. The daughters of Moab seduce the Israelites with bodily pleasures and "strange food" and the Israelites, in turn, eat and "bow down" to Baal.[27]

Read against the grain, the affair of Baal Peor, much like the episode of the Golden Calf, may be seen as an expression of protest against the official demand for total cultural separation, that is, an attempt to redefine the terms of the covenant. Monotheism fervently rejects syncretism and intermarriage as Moses makes clear already in Exodus, in what seems to be a direct reference to the future events in the plains of Moab:

> Lest thou make a covenant with the inhabitants of the land, and they go a whoring after their gods, and do sacrifice unto their gods, and one call thee, and thou eat of his sacrifice; and thou take of their daughters unto thy sons, and their daughters go a whoring after their gods, and make thy sons go a whoring after their gods. (34:15–16)

But what worries Moses is precisely that which the people desire on encountering the inhabitants of the land. They are finally out of the wilderness, released from the dry, rigid routines of desert life, and back to civilization, a new civilization, with new religious practices—and new women. Without hesitation, they plunge into the captivating world they have just discovered and savor its unfamiliar tastes.

Maturity does not bring about the resolution of identity issues. Quite the contrary, the questions of identity that arise at birth—Who am I? Who are my parents? Where do I come from?—resurge at this point with much force, though in a different mode: Whom should I marry? What sort of home should I build? Is syncretism a blessing or a curse? Here, as before, the fashioning of identity is set against the other, but it also reveals an internal fissure between conflicting notions within the Israelite community regarding cultural individuation.

Pinchas and the Priestly Spear

Official monotheism strikes back. God inflicts a plague on the community for clinging unto Baal Peor and demands that the leaders of the apostasy be executed. Moses, however, takes no initiative. It is left to Pinchas the priest, the grandson of Aaron, to be jealous on behalf of God's jealousy (Num. 25:11) and resurrect the official cultural and sexual hierarchies. He does so in an appalling way. On seeing an Israelite man presenting a Midianite woman (from this point on Midianite women replace the daughters of Moab) to his family at the entrance of the Tabernacle, in what sounds like a nuptial ceremony, Pinchas grabs a spear and impales both of them at once. The spear makes its way through their bodies until it reaches the only body part mentioned, the Midianite's *kuvah*, often translated as "belly" but more likely "womb" (the word is related to *nekeva*, "female," "female genitals"). The womb of the other is penetrated with a violent brutality that is meant to put an end to foreign seduction and restore the superiority of monotheism and manhood: a measure-for-measure punishment.[28] Once the spear hits the Midianite's womb, the plague with which God had struck the Israelite camp ceases immediately.

One of the priestly duties was to guard the opening of the Tabernacle to assure that no layperson or outsider encroached on the holy site. In Mesopotamian and Egyptian temples divine guards were placed at the entrance as protection, but within the monotheistic framework the sanctuary was guarded solely by priests. Such guarding is indispensable, as Jacob Milgrom writes, because "illicit contact with sancta produces divine wrath . . . or plague . . . which not only is liable to strike down the sinner but to engulf the entire community as well."[29] And yet more than spatial delimitation between the sacred and the profane is at stake in Numbers 25. Pinchas's spear is meant to reinforce the symbolic boundaries of the community, to suggest that intermarriage is a grave offense against God, endangering the sacredness of the community, its raison d'être.

The entrance to the Tabernacle is analogous in a sense to the threshold of Canaan: it is a liminal zone where fierce cultural negotiations take place. Much as the Israelite man—who turns out to be Zimri Ben Salu, chieftain of the tribe of Shimon—insists on presenting his Midianite bride, the princess Cosbi Bat Zur, by the opening of the Tabernacle so that the community as a whole (not merely his family) witness the bond and consider a redefinition of marital and religious practices, so Pinchas responds on the spot, expressing the conservative, separatist stance of the priestly circles.[30]

The Rise of the New Generation: The Second Census

A new census is carried out at God's command after the plague of Baal Peor, marking a new departure. While the earlier census at Sinai (Num. 1–2) defined the contours of the nation at the time of the primary initiation, when Israel set out to march in the wilderness as a holy assembly with a tabernacle in its midst, the one conducted in the plains of Moab captures the state of the community on the verge of territorialization. In fact, it is primarily a land census meant to determine the number and names of those who are to inherit lots in Canaan. That the census takes place here and not after the conquest of the land proves yet again the relevance of imagining to nation building.[31] Before the actual possession of Canaan, the land must be imagined as concrete inheritance, available for distribution.

A new generation looms out of the list of names. Only the offspring of the desert generation are numbered as heirs. The census indeed makes a point of the fact that no one of the old generation was included in the records: all had perished in the wilderness (perhaps the last ones during the plague of Baal Peor) in fulfillment of God's curse in Numbers 14.

> These are they that were numbered by Moses and Eleazar the priest, who numbered the children of Israel in the plains of Moab by Jordan near Jericho. But among these there was not a man of them whom Moses and Aaron the priest numbered, when they numbered the children of Israel, in the wilderness of Sinai. For the Lord had said of them, They shall surely die in the wilderness. (Num. 26:63–65)

A moment of national rebirth is at stake. At last the curse of wandering meted out by God onto the desert generation may be lifted. No more carcasses are to fall in the desert. A new generation comes forth, giving rise to a hope of a fresh beginning and a reconciliation between the nation and God.[32] Blessings of national prosperity can now take full force in the open horizons beyond the wilderness.

The census allows for a just and impartial apportionment of land: "Unto these the land shall be divided for an inheritance according to the number of names. To many thou shalt give more inheritance, and to few thou shalt give the less inheritance: to every one shall his inheritance be given according to those that were numbered of him" (Num. 26:53–54). The underlying aspiration is that the Promised Land will be a just home, administered according to a progressive legal apparatus, where the many shall have more land and the few less, where every clan shall reside peacefully within the boundaries of its holding.

The power of national imaginings, as Anderson suggests, is to transform "fatality into continuity, contingency into meaning."[33] The death and failures of one generation do not call for an end. Indeed, the most significant difference between national and individual biographies lies in the capacity of the former to transcend death and "glide into a limitless future,"[34] creating continuity at points of clear disjunction. There is always room for another national rebirth, another census, and for hope that the blessings will ultimately be fulfilled in future generations.

The Daughters of Zelophehad

The new generation springs to life fully grown, ready to resume the story of the nation where its parents had stopped. The first new voices to be heard are those of the daughters of Zelophehad. The five women—Mahlah, Noah, Hoglah, Milcah, and Tirzah—come forth to the opening of the Tabernacle and challenge the law that prevents them from inheriting land and preserving their father's memory:

> And they stood before Moses, and before Eleazar the priest, and before the princes and all the congregation, by the door of the tabernacle of the congregation, saying, Our father died in the wilderness, and he was not in the company of them that gathered themselves together against the Lord in the company of Korah; but died in his own sin, and had no sons. Why should the name of our father be done away from among his family, because he hath no son? Give unto us therefore a possession among the brethren of our father. (Num. 27:2–4)

In their eagerness to possess land, the daughters of Zelophehad poignantly represent the stance of a generation that knew neither the fleshpots nor the slavery of Egypt. They crave to settle in what seems to them a promising new world, a world that has the potential to be more egalitarian in its consideration of women's rights. They claim to have nothing in common with Korah and other rebellious members of the desert generation. Their complaint is of a type unheard of as yet. The daughters of Zelophehad are concerned not with the loss of Egypt but with the possibility of losing their portion of land in Canaan, given that they have no brothers and their father has died.

But there is more. One can trace here a new perception of memory. Memory now depends on the preservation of land. The father's name "exists as long as it is attached to the land."[35] Without a holding, it is simply wiped out. The land, then, plays a decisive role in creating continuity between one generation and the next. Zelophehad died in the wilderness, but his name can live on in the Promised Land through his daughters.

God and Moses justify the appeal of the daughters of Zelophehad and grant them their request. The law of inheritance is changed so that daughters may inherit when there are no male heirs.[36] The favorable treatment of Zelophehad's daughters in this context has more immediate implications as well. The scene takes place at the opening of the Tabernacle, at the very place where Pinchas's spear was thrust. It makes clear that there is an alternative to the daughters of Moab and Midian, that there are women with whom one can approach the Tabernacle and cross the threshold of Canaan without provoking divine wrath. The lure of foreign women, however, does not fade away, as the report on the war against Midian indicates.

The War against Midian and the Question of Cultural Virginity

The new generation is commanded to take revenge on the Midianites for their part in the Baal Peor affair. This is its first mission. The census, in fact, is also used for military purposes: to count all able-bodied men (*yotsey tsava*) who are above the age of twenty and capable of bearing arms. The Israelite army suddenly seems to be an organized army of full-fledged warriors, with a fixed number of representatives from each tribe and all the necessary sacred equipment: holy instruments and priestly trumpets (Num. 31:5–6).[37]

To be sure, the men of the new generation are better suited for conquest than were their fathers, but this does not mean that they are innocent of the illicit desires of their precursors.[38] Despite the high expectations, the rise of the new generation entails no distinct spiritual progress.[39] Ironically, the warriors who participate in the battle—under the leadership of none other than Pinchas—take Midianite women as captives, among them the seductive women of Baal Peor.[40] Moses chides them with much anger:

> You have spared every female! Yet they are the very ones who, at the bidding of Balaam, induced the Israelites to trespass against the Lord in the matter of Peor, so that the Lord's community was struck by the plague. Now, therefore, slay every male among the children, and slay also every woman who has known a man carnally; but spare every young woman who has not had carnal relations with a man. (Num. 31:15–18)[41]

This is the first time the Israelites take women captives. They now more clearly resemble the conquering Amorites whose victory song is quoted in Numbers 21. More astounding, they also resemble Pharaoh—sparing the females, murdering the males. But the change in their position, their capacity to take possession both in military and in sexual terms, does not make them less susceptible to the seduction of the other.[42]

Moses finds a curious solution. He draws a distinction between Midianite virgins who may be taken as wives and Midianite women who have "known" men, the assumption being that a virgin is a blank screen bearing no "knowledge," no cultural traces, and thus posing no threat.[43] Is Moses trying to justify his own marriage to Zipporah, the daughter of the Midianite priest Jethro? Is this why he did not respond on seeing the couple by the entrance of the Tabernacle? Intermarriage cannot so easily be rejected—it may be found even in the biographies of the greatest leaders of the nation. David's ancestress, Ruth the Moabite, is another case in point.

The Return of Balaam

When Balaam unexpectedly turns up again in Numbers 31, after a few chapters of absence, we discover that the seer was slain together with the five kings of Midian in the course of the war. At this point he is regarded not as a benevolent other who became God's messenger but as the one who enticed the children of Israel to worship Baal Peor, initiating Israel into the forbidden mysteries of adulthood: "whoredom" and idolatry. We witness here, in Geoffrey Hartman's terms, "the fault lines of a text, the evidence of a narrative sedimentation that has not entirely settled, and the tension that results between producing one authoritative account and respecting traditions characterized by a certain heterogeneity."[44] The biblical redactors did not try to do away with contradictions: they played different traditions against each other, shaping a heterogeneous representation of Israelite history.[45]

Samuel Loewenstamm smooths out the differences between the two accounts of Balaam by suggesting that the seer was an advocate of syncretism—at first he tried to convince the Moabites to accept the monotheistic God and later did the opposite, that is, seduced the Israelites to take part in pagan rites.[46] Whether or not one accepts Loewenstamm's reconstructed plot, it rightly points to the outcome of the juxtaposition of the two accounts: Balaam's hybridity becomes more pronounced. The seer can no longer be regarded as a "convert." He is a man of two cultures and diverse religious affiliations, whose conduct is unpredictable.

How to deal with the other is a question that haunts the nation on the threshold of national adulthood. Can the fascination with the other be fruitful? Can a foreign seer be God's agent? Is it possible to appropriate other customs and traditions without losing one's identity? Is it possible to marry foreign women and "dwell apart" at the same time?

Betrothal on Condition

On the threshold of Canaan, the nation prepares to commit itself to the land, to betroth her, as it were. This match is made in heaven and as such reinforces the covenant between God and the nation. It is a triangular marriage, in which God and Israel share the role of the bridegroom. The metaphor of national betrothal, with its complex familiar dynamics, is elaborated in Isaiah's well-known prophecy of redemption. Speaking to Jerusalem, in a tone of consolation, the prophet assures her:

> Thou shalt no more be termed Forsaken; neither shall thy land any more be termed Desolate: but thou shalt be called Hephzibah, and thy land Beulah: for the Lord delighteth in thee, and thy land shall be married. For as a young man marrieth a virgin, so shall thy sons marry thee: and as the bridegroom rejoiceth over the bride, so shall thy God rejoice over thee. (Isa. 62:4–5)

In Numbers, however, national betrothal is not that hopeful. There is no guarantee that Israel will live in the Promised Land happily ever after under God's auspices. The shadow of exile hovers on the threshold. If Israel fails to erase the traces of previous cultures from the Promised Land, Moses warns, and defiles its home with idolatrous rites of the sort adopted in the plains of Moab, that which God planned to do to the Canaanites will be enacted upon them (Num. 33:56). The Israelites will be dispossessed at once.

Wresting a Blessing

Whether or not Israel is ready to "dwell apart," or deserves a land of its own, it now possesses the password that can open the gates to the promised dwelling. Following the model of Jacob—whose name is evoked numerous times in Balaam's oracles as a designation for the nation—the nation manages to wrest a blessing that would assure its safe entry to Canaan.

Blessings, as Jacob's story amply shows, are not easily granted: they must be wrested time and again through a prolonged process of maturation. The eponymous father first wrests Esau's birthright (the prerequisite for a blessing) in exchange for a pot of lentils, then he wrests a blessing from his blind old father while feigning to be Esau, and finally he wrests a blessing and a new name, "Israel," from a divine being during a nocturnal combat. All these wrestings and wrestlings are relevant to the understanding of the nation's history on the threshold of Canaan, but the latter one particularly so.

The struggle with the divine opponent takes place on the bank of the Jabbok, when Jacob is about to cross the river on his way back to Canaan. It is a fearful night. Homecoming, as always, is a risky and complex move. Esau is waiting on the other side of the river and the question of which of the siblings will assume the father's position and inherit the land is still disturbingly open. Jacob, who is left alone, marked with solitude—the familiar setting apart of the one chosen by God—spends the night wrestling with a mysterious divine being. At the break of dawn, the "man," much like a nocturnal demon, asks to be released, but Jacob refuses to let go unless he receives a blessing. The opponent, whose arm is twisted, complies and grants Jacob the name of the nation: "Israel."

What this final blessing scene suggests is that Jacob needs to wrest a blessing not only from Esau—the other nation—but also from God. This is equally relevant for the nation as a whole. Twisting the arm of the foreign seer in the plains of Moab is only part of the story. Another wrestling—with the ultimate other—may be traced behind it. God, who was ambivalent already at the moment of national birth, is no less ambivalent on seeing the nation's conduct on the verge of adulthood. He is well aware of the "snares" that await the nation on settling in the land and cannot but be worried about future apostasies with other women and other gods. He is jealous as usual—and there is always the temptation of delivering another curse that would defer yet again the fulfillment of His initial promises. God, after all, is a master of cursing—not only of blessing—as the list of curses in Deuteronomy (directed at those who dare violate the covenant) amply shows.

"Am not I thine ass, upon which thou hast ridden ever since I was thine unto this day?" asks the ass, chiding Balaam for lacking trust in her after all these years. Masters, the ass provocatively suggests, may be blind to what goes on in the lives of their subordinates. On the bank of the Jordan God (or is it Moses?) sees the ass's point. If we consider the folkloric ass as representing the vox populi, then we may say that at this liminal station God finally yields to the desire of the members of the new generation for a land of their own and ventures to trust them—for a while at least. He finally approves of the crossing and allows the blessings delivered in Genesis to Abraham, Isaac, and above all to Jacob—the blessings that Balaam reaffirms with much extravagance—to fashion a new map beyond the Jordan River. The waters need to be parted again. There is no way back.

Limping

Israel will end up crossing the river and taking possession of Canaan, leaving the plains of Moab behind. But this national rite of passage, this second initiation, is not a magical coming of age in which the foundling nation suddenly turns into an invincible upright hero and acquires cultural individuation and dominance.

The most relevant image of crossing in this connection is that of Jacob at the Jabbok, after the struggle with the divine messenger. Jacob, as one recalls, limps. "And as he passed over Penuel the sun rose upon him, and he halted upon his thigh" (Gen. 32:31). He limps because the mysterious opponent "touched the hollow of [his] thigh" (32:25). He limps because he is a mortal who has striven with God and one cannot emerge unscarred from such intense intimacy. He limps because mortals lack perfection and have their points of weakness. (Achilles and Oedipus are two other well-known examples.) He limps because scars are a language and this is the mark of chosenness, commemorated by an alimentary taboo to be kept by the children of Israel in days to come. "Therefore the children of Israel eat not of the sinew which shrank, which is upon the hollow of the thigh, unto this day: because he touched the hollow of Jacob's thigh in the sinew that shrank" (32:32).[47] He limps because of the cost of dreams, the cost of growing up, of assuming the father's position.[48] He can hear the cry of Esau, way back, over the lost blessing and feel his own tears piling up, the tears that will burst out in the forthcoming encounter with his brother. He limps while crossing, because even after prevailing in the struggle with the unfathomable "man" he is still not exempt from fear on approaching the border of the Promised Land. He limps because this homecoming is temporary: another exile awaits him and his offspring in the future.

But in the meantime, the sun rises upon him as he passes over the Jabbok and no more adversaries—whether human or divine—block the road.

CHAPTER SEVEN

Epilogue

Mount Nebo

It always felt to me—a wrong
To that Old Moses—done—
To let him see—the Canaan—
Without the entering—

And tho' in soberer moments—
No Moses there can be
I'm satisfied—the Romance
In point of injury— . . .

The fault—was doubtless Israel's—
Myself—had banned the Tribes—
And ushered Grand Old Moses
In Pentateuchal Robes

Upon the Broad Possession
'Twas little—But titled Him—to see—
Old Man on Nebo! Late as this—
My justice bleeds—for Thee!

Emily Dickinson, 597

The essence of wandering in the wilderness. A person, who as leader of his people goes this way, with a remnant (more is unthinkable) of consciousness about what is happening. He is on the trail of Canaan for his entire life; that he should see the

> land only just before his death is incredible. This last prospect could only have the purpose of demonstrating how incomplete a moment human life is, incomplete because this kind of life could go on endlessly and yet would result in nothing other than a moment. Not because his life was too short does Moses not reach Canaan, but because it was a human life.
>
> *Franz Kafka,* Diaries, *1914–1923*

> Well, I don't know what will happen now. We've got some difficult days ahead. But it really doesn't matter with me now—because I've been to the mountaintop. I don't mind. Like anybody, I would like to live . . . but I'm not concerned about that now. I just want to do God's will, and God's allowed me to go up to the mountain. I've looked over and I've seen the promised land. I may not get there with you, but I want you to know tonight that we as a people will get to the promised land. So I'm happy tonight. I'm not worried about anything, I'm not fearing any man. Mine eyes have seen the glory of the coming of the Lord.
>
> *Martin Luther King, Jr., 1968*

I close with Mount Nebo, the locus where the Pentateuch—the primary biography of ancient Israel—ends. From this point on Israel ceases to be a full-fledged character. The voice of the nation is heard on occasion in other historical texts in the Bible, but it no longer assumes a central role in the drama.[1] To be sure, the history of the people continues, but once we move beyond the formative years of the nation into Canaan, once we move beyond the liminal zone of the desert, where the primary questions about the origin and character of Israel are raised with unparalleled intensity, the mythical quality of the narrative subsides and the personification of the nation as God's rebellious firstborn son becomes less elaborate. It is only in the prophetic texts that the nation once again becomes personified extensively, though in a different mode, by means of a different guiding metaphor: the jealous Husband and His lawless wife.

This book focuses on the Father-son relationship, but through its partial exploration of national imagination in the Pentateuch it seeks to shed light on the complex interweaving of individual and collective identities in the biblical text as a whole. Whether ancient Israel is imagined as a son, or a wife—any attempt to understand it, the Bible seems to suggest, requires a plunge into the intricacies of the individual psyche and the tumultuous world of interpersonal relationships.

The nation—particularly in Exodus and Numbers—is not an abstract detached concept but rather a grand character whose biography is intimately connected with a whole gamut of individual histories. Jacob, the eponymous character, who bears the name of the nation, is the most conspicuous example of how the community imagines its embodiment within an individual. But the heterogeneity of the nation depends on a variety of representatives. Fragments of histories as different as those of Moses, Abraham, Isaac, Yocheved, Zipporah, Hagar, and Balaam are also linked to the nation's biography and take part in its construction. In its turn, however, the biography of the nation seeps into the lives of individuals and shapes their desires and destinies, wittingly and unwittingly.

When Moses goes up to Mount Nebo, he goes alone, "solitary

as he has always been, more solitary than he has ever been before," but his final vision is meant to be seen by all.[2]

> And Moses went up from the plains of Moab unto the mountain of Nebo, to the top of Pisgah, that is over against Jericho. And the Lord shewed him all the land of Gilead, unto Dan, and all Naphtali, and the land of Ephraim, and Manasseh, and all the land of Judah, unto the utmost sea. . . . And the Lord said unto him, This is the land which I sware unto Abraham, unto Isaac, and unto Jacob, saying, I will give it unto thy seed: I have caused thee to see it with thine eyes, but thou shalt not go over thither. (Deut. 34:1–4)

From Mount Nebo, Moses can see the power and limits of his dreams, the power and limits of national dreams. He will not cross the Jordan River—death is an aborted rite of passage—but the land of promise (all of it) is right there before his eyes, with its tribal divisions, awaiting the crossing of the new generation. The Bible does not offer the consolation of afterlife but rather a story of national continuity under the vigilance of God. The death of Moses and his generation is not the end of the story. Their dreams are to be pursued by those who follow them, much as they followed in the footsteps of Abraham, Isaac, and Jacob to the land of Canaan.

From Mount Nebo, Moses can see the tremendous journey the nation has made. What a road, what a fate, lie between the times in which the Hebrew slaves were crushed by Pharaonic bondage and the euphoric national revelation at Mount Sinai, between the persecution of the nation by another's law, by Pharaoh's decrees, and the foundation of an independent legal apparatus, between the ongoing thirst and hunger in the wilderness and the discovery of a new promising landscape beyond the desert.

But Mount Nebo provides not only a hopeful glimpse at the nation's future. It marks the unmistakable fissure that lies between revolutionary dreams—dreams of a just society in a bountiful landscape—and their realization. If Moses' "eye was not dim, nor his natural force abated" (Deut. 34:7) at the moment of his death, it is because he can now see not only the fulfillment of his national dreams but also their shortcomings.

Moses is a member of the desert generation, and its critique of national premises is not entirely foreign to him. He realizes, with the ten rebellious spies, that the land of milk and honey may devour its inhabitants, that the fruitful land has its snares, that settling down in Canaan may turn out to be something of a curse rather than a blessing. He realizes, with the other giants of the desert generation, that a land that is "not sown" leaves more room for dreaming than a tilled land whose boundaries are determined via horrifying wars and bloodshed.

In his farewell speech in Deuteronomy, Moses envisions some of the dangers that lie in prosperity:

> And when thy herds and thy flocks multiply, and thy silver and thy gold is multiplied, and all that thou hast is multiplied; Then thine heart be lifted up, and thou forget the Lord thy God, which brought thee forth out of the land of Egypt, from the house of bondage. (8:13–14)

The blindness and arrogance of those who have it all, who take their land for granted, is to be dreaded. Intoxicated by their power, having no memory of the days of bondage or the God who had delivered them, they will bring fearful disasters upon the nation, exile being one of the most agonizing blows.

Standing on Mount Nebo, Moses represents the acute pain of exiles in days to come—those who wander outside their land as well as those who are strangers within—longing for a home where they may thrive freely.[3] On Mount Nebo, Moses represents the power that is needed to go up the mountain and envision a different future even if the Promised Land remains in some way beyond reach.

The story of ancient Israel is a particular narrative that represents the life of a particular community in a given period, and yet it has had the power to shape other collective and individual identities in different lands and different times. How this narrative has managed to transcend national and temporal borders is a baffling question that remains beyond the scope of this project. Let me suggest, however, that if so many communities in the making have adopted the Bible as a narrative base, it is because of the remarkable literary power of this founding text, because it touches on the personal while fashioning the collective, because it offers a daringly profound representation of national formation, where conflicting views of the nation are placed side by side, where exhilarating moments of collective creativity are juxtaposed with moments of immense despair and appalling violence, where the fragility of concepts such as "chosenness" and "promise" is an ongoing concern.

The story of ancient Israel is told and retold already within the biblical text itself. What the differences between the diverse accounts make clear is the unlimited possibilities of imagining a community. The life of a nation is not a fixed entity with fixed characteristics. National biographies, like individual biographies, must be reinterpreted time and again in light of changing perspectives and changing circumstances.

In my own retelling of the story of ancient Israel, I have tried to probe the ambivalent margins of the nation, to seize hold of countermemories, to flesh out the stiff neck of the nation, to highlight the fissures in the text, to evoke the voices of others within the voice of Israel. I believe, with Walter Benjamin, that "to articulate the past historically does not mean to recognize it 'the way it really was.' . . . It means to seize hold of a memory as it flashes up at a moment of danger. . . . In every era the attempt must be made anew to wrest tradition away from a conformism that is about to overpower it."[4]

NOTES

Chapter 1. Introduction

1. All quotations from the Bible are from the King James Version unless otherwise indicated.

2. For more on the figurative language of biblical promises, see the inspiring discussion of Chana Kronfeld (1996: 131–140).

3. Anderson [1983] 1991: 6.

4. Ibid., 204–206.

5. For a similar critique, see Smith 1987; and the introduction by Carla Hesse and Thomas Laqueur to *Representations* 47 (1994): 1–12.

6. Anderson [1983] 1991: 18.

7. Stephen Grosby (1991: 245) offers an interesting analogy in this connection. He suggests that the affiliation with a given god of a given land in ancient nationality is analogous to the conception of citizenship in modern nations.

8. For an extensive discussion of the question of national literature in the ancient Near East, see Greenberg 1969: 12–13.

9. For more on Greek foundation stories, see Malkin 1987, 1994.

10. Gruen 1992: 31.

11. On the comparison between the Bible and the *Aeneid*, see Weinfeld 1993: 1–21; Licht 1980.

12. In *Orlando* Virginia Woolf offers a provocative story about a character named Orlando, who was born as a male child in the Elizabethan period and was transformed, suddenly, into a female character in the eighteenth century. The history of Orlando is inextricably connected with that of England.

13. It is only in the Prophetic texts that the nation is construed as God's wife. For a cogent analysis of the Husband-wife metaphor, see Halbertal and Margalit 1992: 9–36.

14. Much has been written on the anthropomorphic character of God—by scholars as diverse as Ezekiel Kaufmann (1972), Phyllis Trible (1978), and Jack Miles (1995). In most of these cases, however, the concomitant personification of the nation has not received much attention.

15. This is an interesting monotheistic revision of the divine lineage attributed to heroes in polytheistic traditions. No biblical hero could be defined as God's son (that would make Him far too anthropomorphic), but the nation as a whole may acquire such a status precisely because it is more clearly a metaphoric affiliation.

16. Greenberg 1969: 12. For more on the biblical treatment of Israel as a "young" nation, see Funkenstein 1993: 50–53.

17. Funkenstein 1993: 51. See also Yerushalmi 1982.

18. Much has been written on the intricate interrelations of literature and history in biblical narrative. See in particular the insightful studies of Robert Alter (1981); David Damrosch (1987); and Yairah Amit (1997).

19. Regina Schwartz (1997) and James Nohrnberg (1995) are two notable exceptions.

20. Auerbach [1946] 1974: 12.

21. Ibid., 13.

22. Ibid., 23.

23. Freud [1939] 1967: 127.

24. The Egyptologist Jan Assmann provides a fascinating corroboration of Freud's reconstruction of Akhenaten's (Ikhnaton) impact on the Mosaic tradition in *Moses the Egyptian* (1997).

25. Yerushalmi 1991: 34. For more on the question of memory, see Caruth 1996: 10–24.

26. The fluidity of the term is all the more conspicuous in its application to the nation's formative years. "I fell in love with Israel / When he was still a child [*na'ar*]; and I have called [him] My son / Ever since Egypt," says Hosea (11:1) in God's name. The new JPS translates *na'ar* as "child" (much like the King James Version), but one could argue that "infant" and "youth" hover in the background.

27. I rely on Homi K. Bhabha's work in this connection. Bhabha (1994: 139–170) aptly challenges Anderson's emphasis on the stability and coherence of national constructs and calls for a consideration of the "nation's margin and the migrant's exile" (139), that is, for a consideration of the fuzzy borders of the nation. On the question of periodization, however, Bhabha follows Anderson, treating national imagination as a modern phenomenon. Thus he defines the nation "as the measure of the liminality of cultural modernity" (140)—as if exile, migration, and minorities were a modern invention—and relies exclusively on modern literary texts (e.g., Morrison, Gordimer, Conrad).

28. See McCarthy 1978; Sarna 1989: 114–115.

29. Earlier exegetes rely on this link. Thus Radak interprets the different animals as representative of the different exiles—the Egyptian, Greek, and Roman exiles in particular. For more on this topic, see Leibowitz 1981.

30. That the possession of a land depends on moral conduct is made clear in the divine warning of Leviticus 18:28—"That the land spue not you out also, when ye defile it, as it spued out the nations that were before you."

31. I rely on the commentaries of Cassuto ([1944] 1961: 351–354) and Alter (1996: 66).

32. Schwartz (1997: 21–23) reads this scene as another case in which Israel's identity is "forged in violence." She rightly points to the violent dimension of collective identities but here, as elsewhere, fails to consider the empowering aspects of national imaginings, the extent to which they entail a promise of life beyond violence. Bhabha's (1990: 3) perception of the nation as "Janus-faced" is closer to the mark.

33. For more on Israel's birth in exile, see Eisen 1986; Machinist 1991; Gurevich and Aran 1991; Boyarin and Boyarin 1993.

34. On Exodus as a voyage through the other, see de Certeau 1988: 319.

Chapter 2. Imagining the Birth of a Nation

1. For more on the link between the opening of Exodus and the promises and blessings of Genesis, see Cassuto [1951] 1967: 7–9.

2. My analysis of the interrelations between the birth story of Moses and that of the nation is indebted to the insightful observations of James Nohrnberg in "Moses" (1981). Nohrnberg, however, focuses on the representation of Moses rather than of Israel.

3. The midrash noticed this structuring and defined it as *ma'aseh avot siman lebanim*, "the deeds of the fathers are a sign for their children."

4. For more on the interrelations of Abraham's story and the nation's, see Buber 1982: 30–31.

5. I will deal extensively with the relevance of Jacob's story to the nation's biography later on. Hagar's biography challenges the hermeneutic principle "like father, like son" (*ma'aseh avot siman lebanim*). A more appropriate formulation in this case would be "like (m)other, like son." Hagar's otherness is multifaceted given that she is a woman, a slave, a stranger, and the ancestress of the rival Ishmaelite nation. And yet the Bible does not hesitate to reflect on the ways in which her brief biography is tied to the nation's history. As Phyllis Trible (1984: 9–36) and Yair Zakovitch (1991: 26–30) have noted, the textual links between the two narratives are numerous. Much as Hagar, the Egyptian handmaid, was oppressed by her mistress, Sarah, so the Israelites were oppressed as slaves in Egypt (note the recurrent use of the root *'anh* in Gen. 16:6, 9, and in Exod. 1:11–12). Hagar runs off to the desert, and so do the Israelites. The wandering Israelites will indeed follow in her track at points (they too pass through the wilderness of Shur—cf. Gen. 16:7 and Exod. 15:22). In both cases one finds scenes of acute thirst. Hagar's anguish once the water in the skin is gone (she casts Ishmael under a bush and sits crying at a distance, to avoid the sight of her

child's death) seems to prefigure the recurrent cries of the Israelites, who fear their own death and the death of their children by thirst (see Exod. 17:3). In both cases, however, the desert turns out to be a site of divine revelation and intervention. My understanding of exemplary biographies has been sharpened by Sacvan Bercovitch's (1975: esp. 1–34) cogent analysis of biblical typologies in Puritan literature.

6. Biblical scholarship mostly focused on the Mesopotamian version of the "Legend of Saragon," regarding it as a possible source of influence on the biblical writers. The relevant section of the text reads as follows:

> Saragon, the mighty king, king of Agade, am I.
> My mother was a high priestess, my father I knew not . . .
> My mother, the high priestess, conceived; in secret she bore me.
> She set me in a basket of rushes, with bitumen she sealed my lid.
> She cast me into the river which rose not over me.
> The river bore me up and carried me to Akki, the drawer of water.
> Akki, the drawer of water, lifted me out as he dipped his ewer.
> Akki, the drawer of water, took me as his son and reared me.
>
> (Quoted in Sarna [1986] 1996: 30)

One could add another story of Egyptian mythology to the list: that of Horus among the bulrushes. See my discussion on the interrelations of the birth stories of Moses and Horus in *Countertraditions in the Bible* (1992). I will discuss the story of Horus in greater detail in the next chapter.

7. Rank [1914] 1932: 65.

8. Freud [1939] 1967: 9.

9. For more on Freud's description of the "family romance" in *Moses and Monotheism* ([1939] 1967), see Robert 1980; de Certeau 1988; Goldstein 1992.

10. Dorothy Zeligs provides a similar observation in *Moses: A Psychodynamic Study* (1986).

11. For more on the names of the two midwives, see Cassuto [1951] 1967: 13–14.

12. The narrative that best illustrates the humiliating work that the slaves had to endure, I believe, is the story of the straw in Exodus 5. This is the first time Moses and Aaron address Pharaoh. They

ask that he let the Hebrews go for three days into the desert to worship their God. Pharaoh's response is extreme: instead of releasing the Hebrews from work, he increases their workload.

> And Pharaoh commanded the same day the taskmasters of the people, and their officers, saying, Ye shall no more give the people straw to make brick, as heretofore: let them go and gather straw for themselves. And the tale of bricks, which they did make heretofore, ye shall lay upon them; ye shall not diminish ought thereof: for they be idle; therefore they cry, saying, Let us go and sacrifice to our God. Let there more work be laid upon the men, that they may labour therin; and let them not regard vain words. (Exod. 5:6–9)

Pharaoh is the kind of master who is determined to dehumanize his slaves, robbing them of any desire they may have. Any request is deemed a rebellion and is crushed severely. He blames the Hebrews for being idle and sends them off to gather straw for the bricks in addition to their usual tasks. His method of breaking their spirit is excessive, ceaseless work that leaves no room for "vain words."

13. Walzer 1985: 47.

14. *Historia*, 11, 13; quoted in Todorov 1984: 134. The midrash provides a similar story regarding Amram and Yocheved. Amram, according to Shemot Rabbah, refused to have sexual relations with Yocheved due to Pharaoh's decree. It is noteworthy that in other cases of slavery (e.g., North America) the rate of reproduction was very high. In all cases, however, the regulation of reproduction by the masters entailed an appalling dehumanization.

15. Douglass 1960: 833.

16. It is noteworthy that Ezekiel provides a different account not only of the nation's gender but also of its place of birth and primary lineage. "Thy birth and thy nativity is of the land of Canaan," he claims, "thy father was an Amorite, and thy mother an Hittite" (16:3). He regards the Amorites and Hittites (closely connected with the Canaanites according to biblical ethnography) as parent-nations (rather than Egypt) because he is interested in raising a more immediate concern—Israel's distinctiveness (or lack thereof) vis-à-vis the neighboring nations of Canaan. The Exodus tradition, how-

ever, is still present in the scene, for God's second passing by seems to take place in Egypt (see Greenberg 1983).

17. See Nohrnberg 1981: 46.

18. Levine 1977: 40.

19. I am indebted to Walter Benjamin's (1969: 261) discussion on calendars and revolutions.

20. Buber 1988: 75–76.

21. For more on the literary qualities of the Song of the Sea, see Robert Alter's (1985) fascinating analysis.

22. Cassuto [1951] 1967: 177–179.

23. For more on the feminine metaphors of God, see Trible's (1978) groundbreaking work. Trible, however, does not consider the Song of the Sea in this connection. I will explore God's feminine aspects in greater detail in the next chapter.

24. Perhaps God is a cross between the midwives and Pharaoh's daughter.

25. Sarna [1986] 1996: 24.

26. Quoted in Robins 1993: 82.

27. The "Red Sea" is a well-established mistranslation. *Yam suf* actually means "Reed Sea." For more on Miriam's role in this scene, see Dijk-Hemmes 1994: 200–206; Meyers 1994: 207–230.

28. Sarna ([1986] 1996: 37) provides an extensive consideration of the etymology of the name "Gershom."

29. Leibowitz (1981: 31–38) offers an insightful analysis of the various traditions regarding the two midwives.

30. For more on the question of Israel's distinctiveness, see Machinist 1991.

31. Kristeva 1986: 304.

32. Bhabha 1994: 148.

33. Leibowitz 1981: 245.

34. Bhabha 1994: 148.

35. Renan 1992: 19.

36. New JPS translation.

37. Esau is the eponymous father of Edom. "Edom," in fact, is another name for Esau attributed to him (according to Gen. 25:30) for gulping down the red (*'adom*) stew Jacob prepared for him. The

pun, as Alter (1996: 129) suggests, "forever associates crude impatient appetite with Israel's perennial enemy."

Chapter 3. Suckling in the Wilderness

1. For more on feminine imagery and configurations of land, see Kolodny 1975.

2. I am relying on Gay Robins's account in *Women in Ancient Egypt* (1993: 85–90). Interestingly, the power of milk was so highly regarded that it was often mentioned as an item in medical prescriptions. An Egyptian papyrus recommends mixing tips of papyrus, sepet grains, and the milk of a woman who has borne a boy (90).

3. Perhaps her name, "Deborah" (lit., bee), adds a touch of honey to her milk.

4. Trible 1978: 68–69. Trible goes as far as to suggest that the representation of God presupposes that He has a womb and breasts. For more on God's breasts, see David Biale's cogent discussion in "The God with Breasts" (1982), where he analyzes the biblical use of the divine title "Shaddai" (etymologically related to "mountains") and points to the ways in which it is linked by puns to the term for breasts, *shadayim*.

5. Aaron Wildavsky discusses Moses' role in this connection in *The Nursing Father*. Wildavsky (1984: 58) suggests that Moses needs to develop a mode of leadership that would include a feminine principle "if the children of Israel are not to perish as a people." Although the concept "nursing father" serves as the title of Wildavsky's book, he actually says very little about the implications and development of the metaphor in the Bible. For a poetic commentary on Moses as nursing father, see Ostriker 1994: 41–53.

6. Klein [1937] 1975: 325.

7. Klein 1952: 41.

8. Klein was well aware of the wider aspects of her theory. In "Love, Guilt, and Reparation," she devotes a brief section to the ways in which the concept "motherland" may evoke "feelings which borrow their nature from the relation to [one's mother]" ([1937]

1975: 333). For more on Klein's association of weaning with mourning, see "Mourning and Its Relation to Manic-Depressive States" ([1940] 1986). My understanding of Klein's work and its relevance to literature owes much to Elizabeth Abel's insightful book, *Virginia Woolf and the Fictions of Psychoanalysis* (1989).

9. It is left to D. W. Winnicott and W. R. D Fairbairn to add the parental angle to Klein's theory.

10. See Cassuto [1951] 1967: 203.

11. For a similar understanding of the rock as a representation of the Deity in this connection, see Zeligs 1986: 266–285. For the idolatrous quality of rocks, see Gruenwald 1996.

12. For more on the function of repetition in biblical narrative, see Alter 1981; Sternberg 1985.

13. See Milgrom 1990: 448–456, for an extensive and illuminating discussion of the question of magic in this connection.

14. Zakovitch 1990: 64.

15. Note that the word *leshad*, "rich cream," curiously resembles the term for "breast," *shad*, although they are not related etymologically. For more on manna, see Sarna [1986] 1996: 116–120.

16. See Sarna [1986] 1996: 89.

17. The flow of manna indeed stops immediately after the ceremonial crossing of the Jordan River (Josh. 6:12).

18. I am indebted to Ruth Ginsburg for calling my attention to this point.

19. Bhabha 1994: 145–148.

20. For an insightful consideration of the violent pedagogy of the wilderness, see Michael Walzer's reading of the murmurings in *Exodus and Revolution* (1985: 43–70).

21. Anderson 1994: 315.

22. Robins 1993: 86.

23. Marina Warner suggests that the theme of the nursing Virgin, Maria Lactans, probably originated in Egypt, modeled on the representation of Isis suckling Horus. Warner (1976: 192–205) provides a fascinating discussion of the configurations of Mary's divine milk in Christian thought and art.

24. To give but a few more examples: Marduk, the hero of the

Babylonian creation myth, is represented as one who "sucked the breasts of goddesses" (Heidel 1942: 21); the heroic Ysb, in the Ugaritic "Legend of Krt," is the "One who sucks the milk of Asherah / Who suckles the breasts of the Virgin [Anat] / the wet-nurs[es of the gods]" (Gordon 1949: 75); and Ashurbanipal is addressed in an Assyrian text as a privileged king who suckled from the many teats of a divine cow: "Little wast thou, Ashrbanipal, when I delivered thee / to the Queen of Ninveh / Weak wast thou . . . when thou didst sit upon her knees / Four teats were set in thy mouth" (quoted in Neumann 1972: 125).

25. For more on the formation of Roman cultural identity, see Gruen 1992.

26. Freud [1939] 1967: 52.

27. The identification of the Calf with the Egyptian pantheon may be found already in Philo's *Life of Moses.* The people, claims Philo, "fashioned a golden bull in imitation of the animal held most sacred in [Egypt]." Contemporary scholars, however, tend to refute the Egyptian connection. Thus Sarna ([1986] 1996: 218) argues "that it is inconceivable that Aaron and the people could, even for a moment, have identified the God who liberated Israel from Egyptian bondage with an Egyptian deity or have thought of representing Him in a manner characteristically Egyptian." What Sarna neglects to take into account is the dynamics of ambivalence. This is precisely the crux of the scene: the people both want to depart from Egypt and long to return to the land they left behind. In suggesting that the Golden Calf is primarily the product of negotiations with Egyptian culture, I follow the logic of the story. The Israelites, at this point, are not familiar with Canaanite culture. They will encounter Canaanite deities only on reaching the plains of Moab. That the story of the Golden Calf had political implications in later periods (as is evident in the story of Jeroboam's golden calves) need not undermine the primary meaning of the text. Indeed, I follow Cassuto in seeing 1 Kings 12 as an allusion to Exodus 32 and not vice versa (see Cassuto [1951] 1967: 409). For a similar critique, see Walzer 1985: 56–57.

28. For a cogent reading of Jeremiah 2, see Halbertal and Margalit 1992: esp. 17–23.

29. See my *Countertraditions in the Bible*, chap. 4.

30. I provide an extensive reading of Numbers 12 in *Countertraditions in the Bible* (1992: 6–12).

31. For a similar observation, see Trible 1989: 23; Zeligs 1986: 280.

32. Klein ([1937] 1975: 334) mentions the "land of milk and honey" briefly in discussing her theory's relevance to the understanding of the desire to explore new lands.

33. I am indebted to Chana Kronfeld for this observation.

34. For more on the suckling Jerusalem / Zion, see Frymer-Kensky 1992: esp. 168–178. On the role of paradise in the fashioning of cultural identities in Europe, see Olender 1992.

35. I disagree with Shemaryahu Talmon's (1993: 216–254) notion that the desert is never idealized in the biblical text.

36. For a complex reading of the different facets of exile in the Bible, see Eisen 1986: 3–34.

37. de Certeau 1988: 324.

Chapter 4. At the Foot of Mount Sinai

1. See Cassuto [1951] 1967: 223.

2. I have used the new JPS translation in this case.

3. See Buber's (1988: 102) consideration of the ties between the eagles of Exodus 19 and Deuteronomy 32. For more on eagles and the initiation of nestlings, see Ahituv and Ahituv 1962.

4. For an interesting (though brief) consideration of the entire voyage in the wilderness as a single rite of initiation, see Edmund Leach's "Fishing for Men on the Edge of the Wilderness" (1987).

5. The bar mitzvah is one such rite. The ritual can be traced back to the second century C.E.

6. In his groundbreaking work on rites of passage, van Gennep ([1909] 1960) explores different types of ceremonies that mark transitions, primarily those accompanying major junctures in the life cycle—birth, initiation, betrothal, and death. Transitions of this sort, van Gennep suggests, "do not occur without disturbing the life of society and the individual, and it is the function of rites of passage

to reduce their harmful effects" (13) by giving them shape, order, and sanction. Generally, such rites consist of three phases: separation from a given social position, isolation in a liminal (or marginal) state, and aggregation back into society in a new initiated status.

7. In this respect my reading is significantly different from Theodor Reik's consideration of puberty rites at Sinai in *Mystery on the Mountain* (1959).

8. Turner 1969: vii.

9. Ibid.

10. Turner 1967: 105.

11. My understanding of the literary dimension of rites of passage is indebted to Montrose's "'The Place of a Brother' in *As You Like It*" (1981).

12. On the sacred, incest, and prohibitions against touching, see Freud [1939] 1967: 154.

13. The connection between mountains and breasts may be found in the Song of Songs. This is at least one way of reading the beloved's words in 2:8.

14. For more on the interrelations of Moses' initiation rite and that of the nation, see Leach 1987.

15. See Buber 1988: 39.

16. I am indebted to Robert Kawashima's (1996) cogent work for calling my attention to the relevance of Victor Turner in this connection.

17. Turner 1969: 96.

18. Plaskow 1990: 25–27.

19. There is, however, a cryptic trace of another tradition according to which the people went up the mountain after the trumpet "soundeth long" (Exod. 19:13).

20. Buber 1988: 115.

21. The rapid chain of verbs is accompanied by no direct objects that would clarify the nature of the food and drink. This strange juxtaposition of divine revelation and an unspecified feast led the rabbis to assume that the elders were spiritually nourished on seeing the Shekhina (VaYikra Rabbah). The midrash rightly points to the spiritual character of the feast but in so doing ignores the daring mixture of the spiritual and the physical at this point.

22. According to another tradition, God revealed His back to Moses rather than His face:

> Thou canst not see my face: for there shall no man see me, and live. And the Lord said, Behold, there is a place by me, and thou shalt stand upon a rock: And it shall come to pass, while my glory passeth by, that . . . thou shalt see my back parts: but my face shall not be seen. (Exod. 33:20–23)

23. Joyce [1916] 1968: 169–172.

24. On the multiplicity of texts at Sinai, see Nohrnberg 1995: chaps. 2–3.

25. The obsessional commitment to the Text and its interpretation only increases in postbiblical times. See Moshe Halbertal's illuminating discussion in *People of the Book* (1997).

26. For more on the question of national consent, see Walzer 1985: 71–98.

27. Sarna [1986] 1996: 141.

28. Ibid., 158–189.

29. David Damrosch (1987) offers an insightful analysis of the interweaving of law and narrative in the Bible, through a close reading of Leviticus.

30. For a consideration of marking and re-marking in the story of Jacob, see Barthes 1977.

31. See van Gennep [1909] 1960: 74–75.

32. See Eliade 1958: 13–14.

33. New JPS translation.

34. For more on the Calf as an emblem of God rather than as a deity, see Knohl 1995: 23–26.

35. New JPS translation.

36. My reading of idolatry "as a sin within a system of interpersonal relationships" is indebted to the stimulating discussion of Halbertal and Margalit (1992: esp. 9–36) regarding the Husband-wife metaphor.

37. New JPS translation.

38. My understanding of popular religion as an alternative set of religious practices is indebted to the work of Davis (1974, 1982). For more on popular religion in the Bible, see Ackerman 1988.

39. Cassuto ([1951] 1967:414), among others, goes as far as assuming that the people engaged in an orgiastic celebration, of the kind practiced in pagan fertility cults. The biblical account, however, gives no indication that orgiastic revelry took place here and one can hardly imagine that it would spare us the details had the latter occurred. It is only at the last station along the road, in the plains of Moab, that we get a full-blown sexual feast.

40. Bakhtin [1965] 1984: 11–12.

41. I am indebted to Reik's (1931: 314–317) intriguing reading of the Calf as the emblem of the Son.

42. Tosafot, Shabath II, 116a.

43. Ginzberg 1942: 3:242. Quoted in Walzer 1985: 70.

44. Walzer 1985: 97.

45. I am relying on Freud's definition of monotheism as a "father religion" in *Moses and Monotheism.* The exemplary "son religion" for Freud is Christianity. But one needs to bear in mind that the worship of Sons was commonly practiced in polytheistic religions as well (the cult of Horus in Egypt is one such example).

46. Reik 1931: 119–120.

47. For more on the origin of the cherubim, see Cassuto and Barnett 1962: 238–244.

48. Ezekiel develops further the image of the cherubim as divine throne (Ezek. 10).

49. For more on the cherubim and the question of idolatry, see Meltzer 1987: 84–85; Halbertal and Margalit 1992: 48.

50. Josipovici 1988: 96.

51. Translated by Daniel Chanan Matt (1983: 119–120).

52. I take the concept "cultural poetics" from Stephen Greenblatt's *Shakespearean Negotiations* (1988: 4–7).

53. The exact role of the women who assemble at the sanctuary remains unknown. They are mentioned once again in 1 Samuel 2:22. For more on the cultic role of women in ancient Israel, see Meyers 1986: esp. 160. Nehama Leibowitz (1981: 689–695) offers a survey of various commentaries on this verse.

54. Alter 1981: 140.

55. Freud [1939] 1967: 150–151.

56. The history of Israel, for Freud, is part of a broader cultural process. Long ago there was a matriarchal era in which the worship of the great goddess prevailed; with the rise of polytheistic religions this matriarchal order was replaced by a patriarchal one (goddesses were still part of the pantheon but no longer the ruling deities), and finally monotheism with its abstract Father religion appeared on the horizon (with no accompanying goddesses), offering a decisive leap in spirituality. Freud relies here on the highly speculative work of J. J. Bachofen regarding matriarchal orders. For more on Freud, femininity, and religion, see Van Herik 1982.

57. See Kaufmann 1972; Boyarin 1990; Halbertal and Margalit 1992.

58. On displacements in *Moses and Monotheism*, see de Certeau 1988: 308–354.

59. On the separation from the mother in initiation rites, see van Gennep [1909] 1960: 74–75; Eliade 1958: 7–10.

60. Perhaps the femininity of the cloths is enhanced by the expression that depicts the patchwork. The clothes, *yeri'ot* (a feminine noun in Hebrew), are attached to each other, *'isha 'el achota*, literally, "a woman to her sister" (Exod. 26:6).

61. For more on Isis's role as savior, see Bleeker 1963.

62. New JPS translation.

63. I provide an extensive reading of this strange tale in *Counter-traditions* (chap. 5).

64. See Talmon 1954.

65. See Urbach [1975] 1987: 32.

66. Josipovici 1988: 106.

Chapter 5. The Spies in the Land of the Giants

1. Alter 1981: 170–171. For more on Egypt as an underworld of sorts, see Ackerman 1982: 92. Thomas Mann provides an elaborate reading of Joseph's descent to Egypt as a descent to the underworld in *Joseph and His Brothers.*

2. See Natalie Zemon Davis's remarkable rendition and analysis of the story in *The Return of Martin Guerre* (1983).

3. Translated by Robert Fitzgerald. Interestingly enough, the *Odyssey* served as a key text in Greek foundation stories—see Malkin 1998.

4. For more on the question of national home, see Confino's (1997) fascinating discussion.

5. Kristeva 1986: 190.

6. Renan 1992: 19.

7. Hobsbawm 1983: 1–14.

8. For more on the conflicting traditions regarding the origins of Rome, see Gruen 1992.

9. Walzer 1985: 120.

10. Frye 1982: 171.

11. Bradford 1967: 65–66.

12. Greenblatt 1991: 14.

13. Ibid., 76.

14. Quoted in Greenblatt 1991: 76.

15. In Deuteronomy one finds an interesting comparison between Egyptian and Canaanite agriculture: "For the land, whither thou goest to possess it, is not as the land of Egypt, from whence ye came out, where thou sowedst thy seed, and wateredst it with thy foot, as a garden of herbs: But the land, whither ye go to possess it, is a land of hills and valleys, and drinketh water of the rain of heaven" (11:10–11). For more on this topic, see Eisen 1986: 23–25.

16. Numbers Rabbah 16:2, Tanhuma B. Numbers 66.

17. Greenblatt 1991: 136.

18. Interestingly, in the texts of the New World one finds a similar notion of the nakedness of the land. By the 1570s, as Louis Montrose (1993: 179) shows, "allegorical personifications of America as a female nude with feathered headdress had begun to appear in engravings and paintings, on maps, and title pages, throughout Europe."

19. Freud [1908] 1958: 153.

20. My understanding of Freud's use of *unheimlich* with respect to the mother is indebted to Ruth Ginsburg's (1993) cogent discussion of the issue.

21. The notion that the choice of Hebron had something to do

with the burial site of the fathers is evident in Sota 34. According to this tradition, Caleb visited the fathers' graves during the expedition and asked the deceased to help him in his struggle against the other spies.

22. See Talmon 1993: 76–90.

23. See Boling and Wright 1982: 145.

24. In Hebrew one can discern a wordplay between "rope" and "hope," given the double meaning of *tikvah, tikvat chut hashani.* My understanding of Rahab as a "gate of Hope" is indebted to Francis Landy's (1995: 40–41) wonderful reading of Hosea 2.

25. See Greenblatt's (1991: 119–151) discussion on the role of Doña Marina.

26. For more on Rahab's role as other, see Polzin 1980; Fewell and Gunn 1993: 117–121; Rowlett 1996: 176–180.

27. On Rahab's "quoting" of the Song of the Sea, see Alter 1989: 116–118.

28. See Milgrom 1990: 114.

29. Ibid., 115.

30. See Todorov 1984 and Greenblatt 1991 for an extensive discussion on naming and the New World.

31. On the New World as the "blank," "savage" page of European culture, see de Certeau 1988: xxv–xxvi.

32. Baba Bathra I, 73. For more on the tales of Rabbah b. Bar Hana, see Stein n.d.

33. Bialik 1981: 103.

34. Translated by Ruth Nevo (Bialik 1981).

35. On the ongoing ambivalence vis-à-vis the Promised Land, see the thought-provoking discussion of Zali Gurevitch and Gideon Aran (1994).

Chapter 6. Crossing the Threshold

1. On the reference to sibling rivalry in Genesis, see Milgrom 1990: 167.

2. There is usually but one episode per station. The only other station that is allotted much space is Sinai.

3. Bhabha 1994: 5.
4. Eliade 1958: 3.
5. Bhabha 1994: 9.
6. The fantastic quality of Balaam's encounter with an adversary in the course of a journey and above all the talking animal led scholars from Hermann Gunkel (1987) on to regard it as a folktale. My understanding of the role of folktales in the Bible is indebted to Galit Hasan-Rokem's work (1996) on popular traditions in the midrash.
7. On the analogy between Balak and Pharaoh, see Milgrom 1990: 185; Ackerman 1987: 86.
8. Extrabiblical texts attest to the fame of Balaam in Transjordan. In 1967 a Dutch archaeological expedition uncovered fragments of an inscription, dating back to the eighth century B.C.E., on a temple wall located in an ancient delta formed by the juncture of the Jabbok and Jordan rivers (see Milgrom 1990: 473–476). The fragmented text (written in a Semitic language) reveals a story about a seer called Balaam, son of Beor, who learned in a dream that the gods intend to "bolt up the heavens," ordain darkness, and bring famine to the land and death to its inhabitants. Balaam rose on the next day and "wept bitterly" as he related the dire plan of the *shaddayin*, the council of the gods, to the concerned people. Then he interceded on behalf of the people before the fertility gods Shegar and Ashtar. Presumably he was asked to build a temple and found a fertility cult. The inscription ends with the depiction of rain falling and dew dripping (see Rofe 1982; Milgrom 1990).
9. Interestingly enough, the ass has had a prominent role in folk humor around the world from antiquity on. Apuleius's *Golden Ass*, the "Tale of the Donkey" in *The Thousand and One Nights*, and Bottom's dream in Shakespeare's *A Midsummer Night's Dream* are well-known adaptations of such folk traditions. The medieval "feast of the ass," a variant of "the feast of the fools," is another case in point. In his consideration of the popular festive forms adopted by Rabelais, Bakhtin provides a fascinating depiction of the rite. The "feast of the ass," Bakhtin writes, commemorated Mary's flight to Egypt with the infant Jesus.

> The center of the feast is neither Mary nor Jesus, although a young girl with an infant takes part in it. The central protagonist is the ass

> and its braying. Special "asinine masses" were celebrated. . . . Each part of the mass was accompanied by the comic braying "hinham!" At the end of the service, instead of the usual blessing, the priest repeated the braying three times, and the final Amen was replaced by the same cry. ([1965] 1984: 78)

10. Alter (1981: 104–106) provides an illuminating analysis of the theme of "vision" in Balaam's story.

11. Jethro, the Midianite priest, Moses' father-in-law, has an analogous role. Moses defines him as "Israel's eyes" (Num. 10:31)—see Zakovitch 1991: 118.

12. New JPS translation.

13. Eliade (1958: 81–84) provides interesting examples of heroic initiations in men's secret societies that involve magical transformations into wild beasts.

14. The *Iliad* provides similar metaphors for its warriors. Thus Menelaus is likened to a "lion lighting on some handsome carcass / lucky to find antlered stag or wild goat / just as hunger strikes—he rips it bolts it down" (bk. 3, 26–28; trans. Robert Fagles, p. 129).

15. New JPS translation.

16. New JPS translation.

17. For an extended comparison of the story of Balaam and the Garden of Eden, see Savran 1994.

18. Amos offers a similar metaphor (2:9).

19. For a similar observation, see Ackerman 1987: 88.

20. "It was the one who had in the first instance begun the act of whoredom whose daughters ultimately completed the act," claims the midrash, calling to mind the intertextual link between the daughters of Moab and their ancestress, Lot's elder daughter. Having survived the destruction of Sodom, Lot and his daughters hide in a cave near Zoar. The daughters, who think no other man has been left on earth, make their father drink wine so that they may lie with him and have offspring. Two sons, "Moab" and "Amon," are the product of this incestuous scheme. Illicit sexuality marks Moabite history from the very beginning. In the plains of Moab, however, the Israelites take part in prohibited sexual acts, blurring the distinction made in Genesis between the lines of Abraham and Lot.

21. Sexual conduct is no less relevant for the imagining of mod-

ern communities, as George L. Mosse (1985) and Doris Sommer (1991) show.

22. Ackerman 1987: 88.

23. See Buber 1988: 192–193.

24. Hosea provides yet another account of national ripeness and idolatry. In this case, however, the primary metaphor is taken from the realm of fruits: "I found Israel [as pleasing] / As grapes in the wilderness; Your fathers seemed to Me / Like the first fig to ripen on a fig tree. But when they came to Baal-peor / They turned aside to shamefulness / Then they became as detested / As they had been loved" (new JPS, 9:10).

25. On the question of God's jealousy and idolatry, see the insightful discussion of Halbertal and Margalit (1992: 25–26).

26. Venus's response to Cupid's marriage may be seen as a peculiar parallel. On hearing that her son "has been whoring in the mountains," Venus sets out to discover the identity of his mate. His choice of Psyche is perceived as the ultimate offense: "Fine going-on!" she yells at Cupid, "so perfectly in accord with our position in the scheme of things and your good name! First of all, you trample on the express orders of your mother—your queen I should say. . . . More, at your age, a mere boy, entangle yourself in a low lewd schoolboy affair—just to annoy me with a woman I hate for a daughter-in-law" (Apuleius 1962: 126).

In his discussion on divine jealousy, Yehuda Liebes (1996: 7) draws an interesting analogy between Yahweh's jealousy and Venus's jealousy. In both cases, he suggests, jealousy is expressed in personal terms yet entails a religious offense. Cupid's betrayal of Venus is augmented by his choice of a mistaken "object" of worship. See also Liebes 1993.

27. On the seductiveness of "strange women" in the Bible, see Bal 1987: 37–67; Bach 1997: esp. 27–33.

28. Milgrom 1990: 205.

29. Ibid., 342–343.

30. Zimri Ben Salu may be seeking a solution analogous to the Roman one. After a series of gory wars, the Trojans and the Latins reach an agreement that includes a cultural pact (Latin is defined as

the national language) and cross-marriage (Aeneas marries Lavinia, the Latin princess). See the *Aeneid*, bk. 2, 800–840.

31. On the relevance of the census to nation building, see Anderson's fascinating section in *Imagined Communities* ([1983] 1991: 164–170).

32. Dennis T. Olson provides a comprehensive study of the transition between the two generations in *The Death of the Old and the Birth of the New* (1985: 185).

33. Anderson [1983] 1991: 11.

34. Ibid., 12.

35. Milgrom 1990: 231.

36. Walzer (1992: 341) regards the story of the daughters of Zelophehad as an exemplary case for "the accessibility of legal procedures and the popular character of legal argument." The daughters' victory is later compromised when they are required to marry within the clan of their father's tribe (see Num. 36).

37. The substantive legal body that is set up in this war serves as another marker of the institutionalization of the army. The new laws are meant to regulate the distribution of spoils among soldiers, nonsoldiers, and priests, as well as to assure the purification of warriors from corpse contamination.

38. I am indebted to Mieke Bal's cogent discussions in *Death and Dissymmetry* (1988) regarding male heroism and its deconstruction in the biblical text.

39. Most biblical scholars ignore the immediate "fall" of the new generation and construct a coherent history of national progress. Thus Milgrom (1990: 219) suggests that "in contrast to the faithlessness of the generation of the Exodus, the following generation is characterized by fidelity and courage . . . and deemed worthy to conquer the promised land."

40. See the discussion on women captives in Deuteronomy 21:10–15.

41. New JPS translation.

42. This is but the first lapsus in the plan to drive out the Canaanite inhabitants. In the Book of Joshua, as David M. Gunn (1987) points out, the Israelites fail to implement the design of total expul-

sion or genocide (there are different approaches) time and again, the two prominent cases being Rahab (who is incorporated with her entire household within the Israelite camp) and the Gibeonites (who are spared because of their trickery). For more on the different biblical perceptions of conquest, see Weinfeld 1993.

43. For more on the perception of virginity in the Bible, see Bal 1988: 41–46. For a consideration of sexual politics in the war with Midian, see Niditch 1993: 78–89.

44. Hartman 1986: 11.

45. In this case, I would conjecture, they set a folkloric version of a blessed Balaam against a pejorative official account—probably priestly (see Rofe 1982)—of the idolatrous enticer. One may assume that the people, who were fascinated by the culture of the other, sought to recruit the renowned seer on Israel's behalf, whereas the priestly or official circles tried to block cultural borrowings by insisting that a foreign seer could not but be a spokesman for polytheistic cults.

46. Loewenstamm 1965: 135.

47. See Barthes 1977: 135.

48. See Alter's (1996: 183) comment regarding Jacob's limping and the prices "exacted by experience." See also Josipovici 1988: 308–309.

Chapter 7. Epilogue

1. Two prominent examples of later expressions of the vox populi are Joshua 24, where the people commit themselves to the covenant yet again, and 1 Samuel 8, where the elders of Israel demand to have a king that would govern them "like other nations."

2. Buber 1988: 201.

3. See Olson 1994: 17.

4. Benjamin 1969: 255.

BIBLIOGRAPHY

Abel, Elizabeth. 1989. *Virginia Woolf and the Fictions of Psychoanalysis*. Chicago: University of Chicago Press.

Ackerman, James S. 1974. "The Literary Context of the Moses Birth Story." In *Literary Interpretations of Biblical Narratives*, ed. K. R. Gros Louis with James S. Ackerman, 1:74–119. Nashville, Tenn.: Abingdon Press.

———. 1982. "Joseph, Judah, and Jacob." In *Literary Interpretations of Biblical Narratives*, ed. K. R. Gros Louis with James S. Ackerman, 2:85–113. Nashville, Tenn.: Abingdon Press.

———. 1987. "Numbers." In *The Literary Guide to the Bible*, ed. Robert Alter and Frank Kermode, 78–89. Cambridge, Mass.: Harvard University Press.

Ackerman, Susan. 1988. *Under Every Green Tree: Popular Religion in Sixth-Century Judah*. Atlanta: Scholars Press.

Ahituv, Y., and S. Ahituv. 1962. "Nesher." In *'Entsiklopediah Mikra'it*, 5:978. Jerusalem: Mosad Bialik.

Albright, W. F. 1944. "The Oracles of Balaam." *Journal of Biblical Literature* 63: 207–233.

Alter, Robert. 1981. *The Art of Biblical Narrative*. New York: Basic Books.

———. 1985. *The Art of Biblical Poetry*. New York: Basic Books.

———. 1989. *The Pleasures of Reading in an Ideological Age*. New York: Touchstone.

———. 1996. *Genesis: Translation and Commentary*. New York: Norton.

Amit, Yairah. 1997. *History and Ideology in the Bible* [Hebrew]. Tel Aviv: Ministry of Defence.

Anderson, Benedict. [1983] 1991. *Imagined Communities: Reflections on the Origin and Spread of Nationalism*. London: Verso.

———. 1994. "Exodus." *Critical Inquiry* 20 (Winter): 314–328.

Apuleius. 1962. *The Golden Ass*. Trans. Jack Lindsay. Bloomington: Indiana University Press.

Assmann, Jan. 1997. *Moses the Egyptian: The Memory of Egypt in Western Monotheism*. Cambridge, Mass.: Harvard University Press.

Auerbach, Erich. [1946] 1974. *Mimesis: The Representation of Reality in Western Literature*. Trans. Willard Trask. Princeton: Princeton University Press.

Bach, Alice. 1997. *Women, Seduction, and Betrayal in Biblical Narrative*. Cambridge: Cambridge University Press.

Bakhtin, Mikhail. 1981. *The Dialogic Imagination*. Ed. Michael Holquist, trans. Caryl Emerson and Michael Holquist. Austin: University of Texas Press.

———. [1965] 1984. *Rabelais and His World*. Trans. Helene Iswolsky. Bloomington: Indiana University Press.

Bal, Mieke. 1987. *Lethal Love: Feminist Literary Interpretations of Biblical Love Stories*. Bloomington: Indiana University Press.

———. 1988. *Death and Dissymmetry: The Politics of Coherence in the Book of Judges*. Chicago: University of Chicago Press.

Barthes, Roland. 1977. "The Struggle with the Angel." In *Image, Music, Text*, trans. Stephen Heath, 125–141. London: Fontana Collins.

Benjamin, Walter. 1969. *Illuminations*. Ed. Hannah Arendt, trans. Harry Zohn. New York: Schocken Books.

Bercovitch, Sacvan. 1975. *The Puritan Origins of the American Self*. New Haven: Yale University Press.

Bettelheim, Bruno. 1977. *The Uses of Enchantment: The Meaning and Importance of Fairy Tales*. New York: Vintage Books.

Bhabha, Homi K. 1990. "Introduction." In *Nation and Narration*, ed. Homi K. Bhabha, 1–7. London, New York: Routledge.

———. 1994. *The Location of Culture*. London: Routledge.

Biale, David. 1982. "The God with Breasts: El Shaddai in the Bible." *History of Religions* 21 (3): 240–256.

Bialik, Hayim Nahman. 1981. *Selected Poems*. Trans. Ruth Nevo. Jerusalem: Dvir and the Jerusalem Post.

Bleeker, C. J. 1963. "Isis as Saviour Goddess." In *The Saviour God: Comparative Studies in the Concept of Salvation Presented to Edwin Oliver James*, ed. S. G. F. Brandon, 1–16. Manchester: Manchester University Press.

Boling, G., and E. Wright. 1982. *Joshua*. The Anchor Bible. Garden City, N.Y.: Doubleday.

Boyarin, Daniel. 1990. *Intertextuality and the Reading of Midrash*. Bloomington: Indiana University Press.

Boyarin, Daniel, and Jonathan Boyarin. 1993. "Diaspora: Generation and the Ground of Jewish Identity." *Critical Inquiry* 19 (Summer): 693–726.

Bradford, William. 1967. *Of Plymouth Plantation, 1620–1647*. New York: Modern Library.

Brenner, Athalya. 1994. *A Feminist Companion to Exodus-Deuteronomy*. Sheffield: Sheffield University Press.

Buber, Martin. 1982. *On the Bible*. Ed. Nahum N. Glatzer. New York: Schocken Books.

———. 1988. *Moses: The Revelation and the Covenant*. Atlantic Highlands, N.J.: Humanities Press International.

Caruth, Cathy. 1996. *Unclaimed Experience: Trauma, Narrative, and History*. Baltimore: Johns Hopkins University Press.

Cassuto, Umberto. [1944] 1961. *Commentary on Genesis I: From Adam to Noah*. Trans. Israel Abrahams. Jerusalem: Magnes Press.

———. [1951] 1967. A *Commentary on the Book of Exodus*. Trans. Israel Abrahams. Jerusalem: Magnes Press.

Cassuto, Umberto, and Richard Barnett. 1962. "Keruv." In *'Entsiklopediah Mikra'it*, 4:238–244. Jerusalem: Mosad Bialik.

Certeau, Michel de. 1988. *The Writing of History*. Trans. Tom Conley. New York: Columbia University Press.

Childs, Brevard S. 1974. *The Book of Exodus: A Critical, Theological Commentary*. Philadelphia: Westminster.

Confino, Alon. 1997. *The Nation as Local Metaphor: Wurttemberg, Imperial Germany, and National Memory, 1871–1918*. Chapel Hill: University of North Carolina Press.

Damrosch, David. 1987. *The Narrative Covenant: Transformations of Genre in the Growth of Biblical Literature.* San Francisco: Harper and Row.

Davis, Natalie Zemon. 1974. "Some Tasks and Themes in the Study of Popular Religion." In *The Pursuit of Holiness in Late Medieval and Renaissance Religion*, ed. Charles Trinkaus and Heiko Oberman, 307–336. Leiden: E. J. Brill.

———. 1977. "The Historian and Popular Culture." Introduction to *The Wolf and the Lamb: Popular Culture in France from the Old Regime to the Twentieth Century*, ed. Jacques Beauray, Marc Bertrand, and Edward T. Gargan. Saratoga, Calif.: Anma Libri; Stanford French and Italian Studies.

———. 1982. "From 'Popular Religion' to Religious Cultures." In *Reformation Europe: A Guide to Research*, ed. Steven Ozment, 321–341. St. Louis, Mo.: Center for Reformation Research.

———. 1983. *The Return of Martin Guerre.* Cambridge, Mass.: Harvard University Press.

Dickinson, Emily. [1890] 1951. *The Complete Poems of Emily Dickinson.* Ed. Thomas H. Johnson. Boston: Little, Brown.

Dijk-Hemmes, Fokkelien van. 1994. "Some Recent Views on the Presentation of the Story of Miriam." In *Feminist Companion to Exodus-Deuteronomy*, ed. Athalya Brenner, 200–206. Sheffield: Sheffield University Press.

Douglas, Mary. 1993. *In the Wilderness: The Doctrine of Defilement in the Book of Numbers.* Sheffield: JSOT Press.

Douglass, Frederick. 1960. *Narrative of the Life of Frederick Douglass, an American Slave.* Cambridge, Mass.: Belknap Press.

Eisen, Arnold M. 1986. *Galut: Modern Jewish Reflection on Homelessness and Homecoming.* Bloomington: Indiana University Press.

Eliade, Mircea. 1954. *The Myth of the Eternal Return: Or Cosmos and History.* Trans. Willard R. Trask. Bollingen Series 46. Princeton: Princeton University Press.

———. 1957. *The Sacred and the Profane: The Significance of Religious Myth, Symbolism, and Ritual within Life and Culture.* San Diego: Harvest.

———. 1958. *Rites and Symbols of Initiation: The Mysteries of Birth and Rebirth.* Woodstock, N.Y.: Spring Publications.

Exum, Cheryl. 1983. "You Shall Let Every Daughter Live: A Study of Exodus 1:8–2:10." *Semeia* 28: 63–82.

Fairbairn, W. R. D. 1952. *An Object-Relations Theory of the Personality.* New York: Basic Books.

Fewell, Danna Nolan, and David M. Gunn. 1993. *Gender, Power, and Promise: The Subject of the Bible's First Story.* Nashville, Tenn.: Abingdon Press.

Freud, Sigmund. [1908] 1958. "The Uncanny." In *On Creativity and the Unconscious: Papers on the Psychology of Art, Literature, Love, Religion,* trans. John Riviere, 122–161. New York: Harper and Row.

———. [1939] 1967. *Moses and Monotheism.* Trans. Katherine Jones. New York: Vintage Books.

Frye, Northrop. 1982. *The Great Code: The Bible and Literature.* San Diego: Harcourt Brace Jovanovich.

Frymer-Kensky, Tikva. 1992. *In the Wake of the Goddess: Women, Culture and the Biblical Transformation of Pagan Myth.* New York: Fawcett Columbine.

Funkenstein, Amos. 1993. *Perceptions of Jewish History.* Berkeley: University of California Press.

Ginsburg, Ruth. 1993. "The Pregnant Text: Bakhtin's Ur-Chronotope: The Womb." *Critical Studies* 3–4 (1–2): 165–176.

Ginzberg, Louis. 1942. *The Legends of the Jews.* Philadelphia: Jewish Publication Society of America.

Goldstein, Bluma. 1992. *Reinscribing Moses: Heine, Kafka, Freud, and Schoenberg in the European Wilderness.* Cambridge, Mass.: Harvard University Press.

Gordon, Cyrus H. 1949. *Ugaritic Literature: A Comprehensive Translation of the Poetic and Prose Texts.* Rome: Pontificium Institutum Biblicum.

Green, Lyn. 1995. "Evidence for the Position of Women at Amarna." Unpublished paper.

Greenberg, Moshe. 1969. *Understanding Exodus.* New York: Behrman House.

———. 1983. *Ezekiel 1–20.* The Anchor Bible. Garden City, N.Y.: Doubleday.

Greenblatt, Stephen. 1988. *Shakespearean Negotiations.* Berkeley: University of California Press.

———. 1991. *Marvelous Possessions: The Wonder of the New World.* Chicago: University of Chicago Press.

Grosby, Steven. 1991. "Religion and Nationality in Antiquity: The Worship of Yahweh and Ancient Israel." *Archives Européennes de Sociologie* 32: 229–265.

Gruen, Erich S. 1992. *Culture and National Identity in Republican Rome.* Ithaca: Cornell University Press.

Gruenwald, Ithamar. 1996. "God the 'Stone / Rock': Myth, Idolatry, and Cultic Fetishism in Ancient Israel." *Journal of Religion* 76 (3): 428–449.

Gunkel, Hermann. 1987. *The Folktale in the Old Testament.* Trans. Michael D. Rutter. Sheffield: Almond Press.

Gunn, David M. 1987. "Joshua and Judges." In *The Literary Guide to the Bible*, ed. Robert Alter and Frank Kermode, 102–121. Cambridge, Mass.: Harvard University Press.

Gurevitch, Zali, and Gideon Aran. 1991. "Al-Hamakom (Israeli Anthropology)." *Alpayim* 4: 9–44.

———. 1994. "Never in Place: Eliade and Judaic Sacred Place." *Archives de Sciences Sociales des Religions* 87 (September): 135–152.

Halbertal, Moshe. 1997. *People of the Book: Canon, Meaning, and Authority.* Cambridge, Mass.: Harvard University Press.

Halbertal, Moshe, and Avishai Margalit. 1992. *Idolatry.* Cambridge, Mass.: Harvard University Press.

Hartman, Geoffrey H. 1986. "The Struggle for the Text." In *Midrash and Literature*, ed. G. Hartman and S. Budick, 3–18. New Haven: Yale University Press.

Hasan-Rokem, Galit. 1996. *Rikmat Hayim.* Tel Aviv: Am Oved.

Heidel, Alexander. 1942. *The Babylonian Genesis: The Story of Creation.* Chicago: University of Chicago Press.

Hesse, Carla, and Thomas Laqueur. 1994. Introduction. *Representations* 47: 1–12.

Hobsbawm, Eric. 1983. "Introduction: Inventing Tradition." In *The Invention of Tradition*, ed. Eric Hobsbawm and Terence Ranger, 1–14. Cambridge: Cambridge University Press.

Hunt, Lynn. 1992. *The Family Romance of the French Revolution*. Berkeley: University of California Press.

Japhet, Sarah. 1979. "Conquest and Settlement in Chronicles." *Journal of Biblical Literature* 98 (2): 205–218.

Josipovici, Gabriel. 1988. *The Book of God: A Response to the Bible*. New Haven: Yale University Press.

Joyce, James A. [1916] 1968. *A Portrait of the Artist as a Young Man*. Viking Critical Library. New York: Viking Press.

Kaufmann, Ezekiel. 1972. *The Religion of Israel*. Trans. Moshe Greenberg. New York: Schocken Books.

Kawashima, Robert. 1996. "Civil Rites: The Wilderness as National Initiation." Unpublished paper.

Klein, Melanie. 1952. "Weaning." In *On the Bringing Up of Children*, ed. John Rickman, 31–56. New York: Robert Brunner.

———. [1937] 1975. *Love, Guilt, and Reparation and Other Works, 1921–1945*. New York: Dell.

———. [1940] 1986. "Mourning and Its Relation to Manic-Depressive States." In *The Selected Melanie Klein*, ed. Juliet Mitchell, 146–174. New York: Free Press.

Knohl, Israel. 1995. *The Many Faces of the Monotheistic Religion* [Hebrew]. Tel Aviv: Ministry of Defence.

Kolodny, Annette. 1975. *The Lay of the Land: Metaphor as Experience and History in American Life and Letters*. Chapel Hill: University of North Carolina Press.

Kristeva, Julia. 1986. "Women's Time." In *The Kristeva Reader*, ed. Toril Moi, 187–213. New York: Columbia University Press.

Kronfeld, Chana. 1996. *On the Margins of Modernism: Decentering Literary Dynamics*. Berkeley: University of California Press.

Landy, Francis. 1995. *Hosea*. Sheffield: Sheffield Academic Press.

Leach, Edmund. 1983. "Why Did Moses Have a Sister?" In *Structuralist Interpretations of Biblical Myth*, 33–67. Cambridge: Cambridge University Press.

———. 1987. "Fishing for Men on the Edge of the Wilderness." In *The Literary Guide to the Bible*, ed. Robert Alter and

Frank Kermode, 579–599. Cambridge, Mass.: Harvard University Press.

Leibowitz, Nehama. 1981. *Studies in Shemot.* Trans. Aryeh Newman. Jerusalem: Ahva Press.

Levine, Baruch. 1993. *Numbers 1–20.* The Anchor Bible. Garden City, N.Y.: Doubleday.

Levine, Lawrence. 1977. *Black Culture and Black Consciousness: Afro-American Folk Thought from Slavery to Freedom.* New York: Oxford University Press.

Licht, Jacob. 1980. "Te'anat ha-kinun ha-mikra'it." *Shenaton Lemikra ve-lecheker ha-mizrach ha-kadum* 4: 98–125.

Liebes, Yehuda. 1993. *Studies in Jewish Myth and Jewish Messianism.* Trans. Batya Stein. Albany: State University of New York Press.

———. 1996. "Yahadut umitos." *Dimuy* 14 (Winter): 6–14.

Loewenstamm, Samuel E. 1965. "Bil'am." In *'Entsiklopediah Mikra'it,* 2:133–135. Jerusalem: Mosad Bialik.

McCarthy, Dennis. 1978. *Treaty and Covenant: A Study in Form in the Ancient Oriental Documents and in the Old Testament.* Rome: Biblical Institute Press.

Machinist, Peter. 1991. "Distinctiveness in Ancient Israel." *Studies in Assyrian History and Ancient Near East Historiography Presented to Hayim Tadmor,* ed. Mordechai Cogan and Israel Eph'al. Vol. 33 of *Scripta Hierosolymitana.* Jerusalem: Magnes Press.

Malkin, Irad. 1987. *Religion and Colonization in Ancient Greece.* Leiden: E. J. Brill.

———. 1994. *Myth and Territory in the Spartan Mediterranean.* Cambridge: Cambridge University Press.

———. 1998. *The Returns of Odysseus: Colonization and Ethnicity.* Berkeley: University of California Press.

Matt, Daniel. 1983. *Zohar: The Book of Enlightenment.* New York: Paulist Press.

Meltzer, Françoise. 1987. *Salome and the Dance of Writing: Portraits of Mimesis in Literature.* Chicago: University of Chicago Press.

Meyers, Carol. 1986. *Discovering Eve: Ancient Israelite Women in Context.* New York: Oxford University Press.

———. 1994. "Miriam the Musician." In *Feminist Companion to*

Exodus-Deuteronomy, ed. Athalya Brenner, 207–230. Sheffield: Sheffield University Press.

Miles, Jack. 1995. *God: A Biography*. New York: Vintage Books.

Milgrom, Jacob. 1990. *Numbers: The JPS Torah Commentary*. Philadelphia: Jewish Publication Society of America.

Montrose, Louis. 1981. "'The Place of the Brother' in *As You Like It:* Social Process and Comic Form." *Shakespeare Quarterly* 32:28–54.

———. 1993. "The Work of Gender in the Discourse of Discovery." In *New World Encounters*, ed. Stephen Greenblatt, 177–217. Berkeley: University of California Press.

Moore, M. S. 1990. *The Balaam Traditions: Their Character and Development*. Atlanta: Scholars Press.

Mosse, George L. 1985. *Nationalism and Sexuality: Respectability and Abnormal Sexuality in Modern Europe*. New York: Howard Fertig.

Neumann, Eric. 1972. *The Great Mother*. Princeton: Princeton University Press.

Niditch, Susan. 1993. *War in the Hebrew Bible: A Study in the Ethics of Violence*. New York: Oxford University Press.

Nohrnberg, James. 1981. "Moses." In *Images of Man and God: Old Testament Short Stories in Literary Focus*, ed. Burke O. Long, 35–57. Sheffield: Almond Press.

———. 1995. *Like unto Moses: The Constituting of an Interruption*. Bloomington: Indiana University Press.

Olender, Maurice. 1992. *The Languages of Paradise: Race, Religion, and Philology in the Nineteenth Century*. Trans. Arthur Goldhammer. Cambridge, Mass.: Harvard University Press.

Olson, Dennis T. 1985. *The Death of the Old and the Birth of the New*. Chico, Calif.: Scholars Press.

———. 1994. *Deuteronomy and the Death of Moses: A Theological Reading*. Minneapolis: Fortress Press.

Ostriker, Alicia. 1994. "The Nursing Father." In *Out of the Garden: Women Writers on the Bible*, ed. Christina Buchmann and Celina Spiegel, 41–53. New York: Fawcett Columbine.

Pardes, Ilana. 1992. *Countertraditions in the Bible: A Feminist Approach*. Cambridge, Mass.: Harvard University Press.

Plaskow, Judith. 1990. *Standing against Sinai: Judaism from a Feminist Perspective*. San Francisco: Harper and Row.

Polzin, Robert. 1980. *Moses and the Deuteronomist: A Literary Study of the Deuteronomic History*. New York: Seabury Press.

Rank, Otto. [1914] 1932. *The Myth of the Birth of the Hero*. Trans. Mabel E. Moxon. New York: Vintage Books.

Rashkow, Ilona N. 1993. *The Phallacy of Genesis: A Feminist Psychoanalytic Approach*. Literary Currents in Biblical Interpretations. Louisville, Ken.: John Knox Press.

Raz-Kakotskin, Amnon. 1993. "Exile within Sovereignty" [Hebrew]. *Teoria u-Vikoret* 4 (Fall): 23–54.

Reik, Theodor. 1931. *Ritual: Psycho-Analytic Studies*. International Psycho-Analytical Library, no. 19, ed. Ernest Jones. London: Hogarth Press.

———. 1959. *Mystery on the Mountain: The Drama of the Sinai Revelation*. New York: Harper & Brothers.

Renan, Ernest. 1992. "What Is a Nation?" In *Nation and Narration*, ed. Homi K. Bhabha, 8–22. London: Routledge.

Robert, Marthe. 1980. *Origins of the Novel*. Bloomington: Indiana University Press.

Robins, Gay. 1993. *Women in Ancient Egypt*. Cambridge, Mass.: Harvard University Press.

Rofe, Alexander. 1982. *Sefer Bil'am*. Jerusalem: Simor.

Rowlett, Lori L. 1996. *Joshua and the Rhetoric of Violence: A New Historicist Analysis*. Sheffield: Sheffield University Press.

Sarna, Nahum M. 1989. *Genesis*. Philadelphia: Jewish Publication Society of America.

———. [1986] 1996. *Exploring Exodus: The Origins of Biblical Israel*. New York: Schocken Books.

Savran, G. 1994. "Beastly Speech: Intertextuality, Balaam's Ass and the Garden of Eden." *Journal for the Study of the Old Testament* 64: 33–55.

Schwartz, Regina. 1997. *The Curse of Cain: The Violent Legacy of Monotheism*. Chicago: University of Chicago Press.

Smith, Antony. 1987. *The Ethnic Origins of Nation*. Oxford: Basil Blackwell.

Sommer, Doris. 1991. *Foundational Fictions: The National Romances of Latin America*. Berkeley: University of California Press.

Stein, Dinah. n.d. "Devarim Sh-ro'im misham lo ro'im mikan." *Jerusalem Studies in Hebrew Literature* (forthcoming).

Sternberg, Meir. 1985. *The Poetics of Biblical Narrative: Ideological Literature and the Drama of Reading.* Bloomington: Indiana University Press.

Talmon, Shemaryahu. 1954. "Hatan Damim." *Eretz Yisrael* 3: 93–95.

———. 1993. *Literary Studies in the Hebrew Bible: Form and Content.* Jerusalem: Magnes Press.

Todorov, Tzvetan. 1984. *The Conquest of America: The Question of the Other.* Trans. Richard Howard. New York: Harper Perennial.

Trible, Phyllis. 1978. *God and the Rhetoric of Sexuality.* Philadelphia: Fortress Press.

———. 1984. *Texts of Terror: Literary-Feminist Readings of Biblical Narratives.* Philadelphia: Fortress Press.

———. 1989. "Bringing Miriam Out of the Shadows." *Bible Review* 5: 14–25.

Turner, Victor. 1967. *The Forest of Symbols: Aspects of Ndembu Ritual.* Ithaca: Cornell Paperbacks.

———. 1969. *The Ritual Process: Structure and Anti-Structure.* Ithaca: Cornell University Press.

Urbach, E. E. [1975] 1987. *The Sages.* Cambridge, Mass.: Harvard University Press.

van Gennep, Arnold. [1909] 1960. *The Rites of Passage.* Trans. Monika B. Vizedom and Gabrielle L. Caffee. Chicago: University of Chicago Press.

Van Herik, Judith. 1982. *Freud on Femininity and Faith.* Berkeley: University of California Press.

Walzer, Michael. 1985. *Exodus and Revolution.* New York: Basic Books.

———. 1992. "The Legal Codes of Ancient Israel." *Yale Journal of Law and the Humanities* 4 (2): 335–349.

Warner, Marina. 1976. *Alone of All Her Sex: The Myth and Cult of the Virgin Mary.* New York: Vintage Books.

Weinfeld, Moshe. 1993. *The Promise of the Land: The Inheritance of the Land of Canaan by the Israelites.* Berkeley: University of California Press.

Westermann, Claus. [1976] 1980. *The Promises to the Fathers: Studies on the Patriarchal Narratives.* Trans. David E. Green. Philadelphia: Fortress Press.

Wildavsky, Aaron. 1984. *The Nursing Father: Moses as a Political Leader.* Birmingham: University of Alabama Press.

Winnicott, D. W. 1965. *The Maturational Process and the Facilitating Environment.* New York: International Universities Press.

———. 1971. *Playing and Reality.* Middlesex, England: Penguin.

Yerushalmi, Yosef Hayim. 1982. *Zakhor: Jewish History and Jewish Memory.* Seattle: University of Washington Press.

———. 1991. *Freud's Moses: Judaism Terminable and Interminable.* New Haven: Yale University Press.

Zakovitch, Yair. 1990. *The Concept of the Miracle in the Bible.* Trans. Shmuel Himelstein. Tel Aviv: MOD Books.

———. 1991. *"And You Shall Tell Your Son . . . ": The Concept of the Exodus in the Bible.* Jerusalem: Magnes Press.

Zeligs, Dorothy. 1986. *Moses: A Psychodynamic Study.* New York: Human Sciences Press.

INDEX

Compositor: G & S Typesetters, Inc.
Text: 10/15 Janson
Display: Janson
Printer and Binder: Haddon Craftsmen